D0796655

African Americans' Health Care Practices, Perspectives, and Needs

Randolph K. Quaye

UNIVERSITY PRESS OF AMERICA,® INC.
Lanham • Boulder • New York • Toronto • Oxford

Copyright © 2005 by
University Press of America,® Inc.
4501 Forbes Boulevard
Suite 200
Lanham, Maryland 20706
UPA Acquisitions Department (301) 459-3366

PO Box 317
Oxford
OX2 9RU, UK

Library of Congress Control Number: 2004114189
ISBN 0-7618-3023-5 (paperback : alk. ppr.)

Contents

Preface

For the past decade, my research has focused primarily on health and illness and the sociology of developing countries. Within the past five years, I have concentrated on health and illness in the United States, Sweden and Africa. I have tried in my research to further our general understanding of the ways in which cultures interact, and how new and emerging health finance modalities are increasingly shaped by international and national politics. My extensive research of European health care systems has left me wondering what will it take for this nation to give to African Americans what they truly deserve in health care. Why is the U.S. health care system so expensive and unresponsive to the needs of the most vulnerable groups in the country?

Recent reports on U.S. infant mortality rates and life expectancy are disturbing demonstrations of inequalities in the health care delivery system in the United States.

African Americas' Health Care Practices, Perspectives, and Needs emphasizes the fact that an appropriate understanding of the health and health behavior of African Americans requires specific attention to the ways in which social structure shapes the beliefs and behaviors of individuals.

In writing about *the African Americans' health care practices, perspectives and needs,* I have attempted to fill gaps in the sociological literature on health, culture and economics. I take the position that this nation has not done much for African Americans despite several decades of research documenting the wide disparities in health care access and utilization. To do nothing now, is to risk the lives of millions of African Americans.

My work was supported by the New York African American Foundation and The College of Wooster's Faculty Development Fund. Chapter One has appeared in slightly different form in the Journal of Black Scholar. Chapter

Three has appeared in a modified version in the Journal of Multicultural Nursing and Health. I thank both editors for the permission to reprint these two articles.

My thanks are due to many people. Asi, Kwesi, Kofi, Kojo and Kobina for their forbearance while researching and writing this book. I certainly acknowledge the guidance and support from Martha Huggins, Malcolm Willison, Josephine Wright, Alphine Jefferson, Yvonne Williams, Hayden Schilling and Nick Kardulias. A special thanks to my father, Daniel Quaye, my brother, Daniel Quaye Jr., and my mother, Dora Bonney. Thank you all for believing and sticking with me through the years.

June 2004

Introduction

Health care of the highest quality is what one should expect to receive in the United States. After all, the United States spends 14 percent of its Gross Domestic Product on health care services (Kuttner, 1999). If inequalities exist in the distribution and utilization of American health services, the consequences can be expected to be disastrous yet for the nation in both the short term and long run.

Indeed, recent reports on U.S. infant mortality rates and life expectancy are disturbing demonstrations of inequalities in the health delivery system in the United States. Life expectancy for African Americans has lagged behind whites (74.8 years) falling from 69.7 years in the early 1980s to 68.2 years in 2002 (Aguirre & Turner, 2004).

This book attempts to address the impact of poverty and difficult socioeconomic conditions on African-Americans health, as a primer on health inequalities among U.S. minorities, using the disciplines of sociology and of health and ethnic studies. Drawing on current debates about health care access and case studies, along with recent scholarship on African-American health, the health status of African-Americans in general as well as conditions specifically in Albany and in Schenectady County in upstate New York and in three Boston neighborhoods are presented. The subject is very timely, given the current debates on U.S. health care financing and lack of health coverage and under-utilization of health services by the poor. As Congress pursues overhaul of both the Medicaid and Medicare programs, the impact of their failures for the already precarious health situation of the American poor is discussed as well as the need to focus more attention on the effects of economic marginalization, poverty, and discrimination on African Americans' access to good health. The book is written in accessible language and is organized to make it suitable as a reference work as well as a text. It is divided into five chapters. Chapter One contextualizes health care issues such as their worsening infant mortality rates and low life expectancy as trends reflecting unequal income, occupation and education opportunities in the United States. Chapter Two reviews the health problems and services faced by African Americans and explains the important connections between poverty, discrimination, and ill-health. Chapter Three investigates health-seeking patterns among low-income African Americans in particular Boston neighborhoods and in New York's Schenectady and Albany counties. The fourth chapter examines perceptions by health-care providers in Schenectady and Albany on the access and quality of health care for African Americans. The book concludes with a summary of key themes of the book and offers strategies for overcoming African Americans' poor health, including the role of the African-American church as a health-promoting institution in the wider African-American community.

Many citizens wonder what will happen to them and their families should they become unemployed or disabled. For the old, high medical costs, particularly for prescription drugs are eating away at their savings. A recent study suggests that for the majority of Americans, the likelihood of being uninsured for part of any given year is substantial, and family members increasingly worry about their inability to afford health care (Alliance for Health Reform, 2004). If health insecurity is true for whites and the lower to upper middle class, what of African Americans, who traditionally have weaker connections to the labor market and more experience of persistent poverty and discrimination?

Assuming that the goal of health services is to promote health and thereby improve the quality of life of all citizens, can this be said to be true for African Americans? It is the contention of this book that the health care status of African Americans is a function of their marginal position in the U.S. economy and a direct result of both their poverty and widespread discrimination against them. In fact, African Americans are twice as likely as whites with the same income to be without a regular source of care and to identify only a hospital outpatient department or emergency room as their primary source for physician visits. Significantly enough the book suggests that the implementation of race-specific policies that address particular problems faced by African Americans is critical to getting at the root of health care inequalities in the United States. Since race has been and continues to be a significant factor in health care delivery services, any proposed health program that addresses the inequities of class without also considering the differential effects of race will effectively marginalize, as it does now, the health needs of the large U.S. population of poor African Americans.

Chapter One

African Americans in the U.S. Economic System

Thirty-five years after the Kerner Report, the gaps in income between African Americans and the rest of the American population remain as wide as they were in 1960. In fact the U.S. Census Bureau in 2003 reported that poverty had increased significantly since 1970 among African Americans compared to the population as a whole (Armas, 2003). At the same time, child poverty in the United States rose from 11.7 million in 2001 to 12.1 million in 2002. As of 1990, twenty-four percent of African Americans income was below the poverty level and half of African-American children under age six lived in poverty, as compared with 17 percent of white children across the country. The increase in African-American female headed households has been inextricably tied to the feminization of poverty, that is, 51.8 percent of African American families with children under 18 years are headed by women (Schiller,1998). Nowhere is this inequality exposed more powerfully than in the area of African-American health. As already stated, infant mortality rates and life expectancy are clear demonstrations of unequal distribution of health and of health care delivery system in the United States. African–American babies are twice as likely as white babies to die before their first birthday. Being overweight is a problem for 44 percent of African-Americans women aged 20 years and older and diabetes is 33 percent more common among African Americans than among whites. African American babies are twice as likely as white babies to die before their first birthday. Poor nutrition and tobacco smoking are more common among African American than among white with low incomes (National Health Interview Survey,1990:3).

It is further reported that African Americans make fewer annual physician check-ups than do whites and that pregnant African-American women are twice as likely as whites to receive no health care at all, or to receive care only in the last trimester of their pregnancies (Cockerham, 2004). Hospital emergency rooms are the usual port of entry to the medical care system for 20 percent of African Americans compared with 13 percent of whites; emergency room users are more often of low socioeconomic status (White-Means and Thornton, 1989). Patients who use emergency rooms report long waiting lines and discontinuity of care (Quaye, 1994). It has also been documented that patients receiving medical treatment from public hospitals reported less satisfaction with the treatment they received than those using private hospitals (Ell et al. 1994). Significantly in 1997, 21.5 percent of African Americans had no medical insurance as compared with 15 percent of whites (Kuttner,1999). These issues will be discussed in more detail in Chapter 2.

These barriers to care and to paying its cost play a crucial role in the low utilization of health services by African Americans. Limited access to medical care forces African Americas to rely upon folk medicine. Bailey found in his study of Detroit African Americans treatment patterns that some used home remedies, religion and non-prescription drugs to treat their ailments (Bailey,1991). In most cases, these treatments do not relieve the conditions of the sick, but rather exacerbate their condition. This will be discussed in Chapter 3.

Ignoring the impact of medical insurance and focusing primarily on the blatant discrimination, African Americans are shortchanged in the overall health care delivery system. In a study by (Schulman et al.1999: 624) the authors report that "A patient's race and sex may influence a physician's recommendation with respect to cardiac catheterization, regardless of the patient's clinical characteristics." They attribute this to the biases and prejudices of physicians. In another study, "Effects of Race and Income on Mortality and Use of Services among Medicare Beneficiaries" (Gornick et al. 1996) reported that African Americans were provided 17 common procedures less often than whites. Specifically, they determined that "amputation of all or part of the lower limb was 3.6 times as frequent among Blacks than whites and that in 62 percent of amputation, the principal diagnosis was diabetes mellitus, yet diabetes is only 1.7 times more prevalent in elderly blacks than in whites" (791). Early hospital discharge rates for diabetes were 14 percent higher among blacks than among whites. In a similar study, Berger (1993), comparing the use of 32 procedures by African-American and white patients, noted that whites were more likely to receive a higher number of services and better access to higher technology and more modern medical procedures than African Americans. They concluded that the "effect of a patient's race on physicians' institutional decision making may be another important cause for this situation (Berger, 1993:430).

The 1986 Report of the Task Force on Organ Transplantation acknowledged that African Americans are neither transplanted nor represented on kidney transplant waiting lists in numbers that reflect their proportion of the population on dialysis Arnason,1991).

Arnason adds that African Americans wait twice as long for a first transplant than whites (Arnason, 1991). Twelve percent of diabetic white patients but only six percent of African American patients receive a kidney transplant (Arnason,1991). This rate is even more disheartening given the fact that end-stage renal disease is four times higher among African Americans than among whites (Kasiske, 1991).

Even after receiving a kidney transplant, it was found that African Americans experience a 10 to 20 percent lower success rate than whites (Arnason, 1991). This is most probably due to insufficient care at the time of organ transplantation. Perdue and Teraski (1982) found that this variation in successful kidney graft rates between African-American and white patients could be accounted for by the fact that transplant centers with poorer results served a greater number of African Americans. In other words, African American patients were more likely to go to hospitals with less specialized and poorer quality care than whites.

All told, the mortality rates for African Americans have worsened over the past two decades. The question then is, what are the social determinants of African American health? While poverty and the poor socio-economic circumstances of African Americans account for some of their many health problems, the National Health Interview Survey reported that "If the socio-economic effects are set aside, disparities experienced by African Americans and the rest of the population will [still] be observed."(National Health Interview Survey, 1990:2) Simply put, the report stated that "Differences in survival and health between African Americans and whites are not solely explained by poverty, but by unique experiences and cultural orientations of African Americans" (National Health Interview Survey, 1990:32). Blendon (1989) in a recent study suggested that it is differences in ethnic-related lifestyles which account for the disparity in health care utilization among whites and African Americans. Such a view suggests the culture of poverty thesis.

A BLACK CULTURE OF POVERTY:
DOES IT EXIST IN AMERICA?

The "Culture of Poverty" perspective proposes that the state of African-American health is a direct result of disorganized families that have become increasingly isolated socially, economically, and politically from mainstream patterns and norms of behavior (Wilson, 1987:8). As Wilson points out, "Large segments of African Americans live in communities populated primarily by others as poor as themselves; they experience long-term unemployment and are characterized by very long spells of endemic poverty". In general, this viewpoint characterizes African Americans as plagued by high rates of family disruption, female-headed families, joblessness, low educational achievement and work skills; patterns of behavior and attitudes associated with a life of casual work (Auletta, 1982; Wilson, 1987). This perspective also points to low utilization of health services by African Americans as a direct result of their marginality, alienation, and skepticism about medical care (Wallace, 1990). However, as so eloquently critiqued by Wallace, these cultural analyses do not go beyond the behaviors of individuals by which "black culture" and/or a "culture of poverty" held by African-American individuals is used in conjunction with their other risk factors to explain their health inequalities. Subsequent studies by Manton, Patrick and Johnson (1987) have exposed the hypocrisy and the systematic patterns of discrimination that African Americans face in their access to health care. Jackson (1988) concluded in her study that the cultural approach typically overlooks the social determinants of individual behaviors, such as the influence of class status on health conditions as hypertension and obesity. Even when controlled for their so-called unhealthy behaviors, African Americans usually have higher death rates than whites (Manton et al. 1987).

The culture of poverty thesis provides, as most ideological pseudo-scientific theories have done in the past, the "spark" for blaming the victim and for the victims self-blame, by rationalizing the social injustice and discrimination that African Americans continue to experience in health care. The cultural analysis fails to analyze the institutional patterns in the current U.S health care system (Wallace, 1990). In response to such critiques, class and race analysis are given greater credence in this book as important variables for explaining the health disparities between African Americans and the rest of the population. It is to these theoretical issues on class that we turn.

ECONOMIC CLASS AND AFRICAN-AMERICAN HEALTH

In examining the relationship between class and the health of African Americans, class is defined by one's relationship to the means of production. In this important sense, production is central to social life (Gilbert and Kahl, 1993). In "Class, Status, and Party, Weber offered an inclusive approach for investigating social standing in society. Weber defined "class" on the basis of the economic opportunities an individual has in the labor, commodity, and credit markets (Weber, 1947:186). Status standing, by contrast, is determined by the specific positive or negative social estimation of its honor. Thus, "classes are stratified according to their relationship to the production and acquisition of goods, while status groups are stratified according to the principles of their consumption of goods as represented by special styles of life" (Weber, 1947:186).

Be that as it may, we propose that African-Americans access to health care insurance and health care utilization is explained by their relationship to the production and acquisition of goods, not to their lifestyle, that is, their culture. To explore the linkage between class and health, the impact of the economy on African Americans must be discussed. Health status differentials are affected by life opportunities and socio-economic conditions far more than by the nature and quality of medical care itself. In other words, economic discrimination and resulting poverty are proposed as the major factors influencing African American status and participation in the American health care system, and their utilization of that system. In 1997, 21.5 percent of African Americans were medically uninsured, a rate one and half times that of whites (Kuttner, 1999). And of course, employment status and occupation play a role in the likelihood of being uninsured for all or part of a year. It is remarkable that in a recent study, about eighty-five percent of the uninsured African Americans were either working or were family members of workers (Friedman, 1991). Structural inequality (such as the exceptionally high percentage of African Americans in poverty), a direct result of racial discrimination, leads to greater African-American under representation in high-status professional, technical, and managerial positions. They are, however, over-represented in service occupations. Table 1 compares non Hispanic whites and blacks.

Table 1.　Distribution of African Americans and Non-Hispanic Whites Occupational, 2000

	Whites	African Americans
Managerial and professional	33.2%	21.7%
Technical, sales	30.3%	29.9%
Services	11.8%	22.6%
Operations, laborers	11.6%	19.1%
Farming, forestry, fishing	2.3%	0.8%

Source: U.S. Bureau of the Census, 2002; Population Statistics and Demographics.

Since 1970, the income gap separating African Americans and whites has widened. The proportion of white families making $50,000 or more a year

increased from 24.1% in 1970 to 32.5% in 1990, more than a fifty percent increase. Among African Americans, incomes above $50,000 annually in-
creased from 9.9% in 1970 to 14.5% in 1990, only a 46.5 percent rise (Yetman,1991).

One of the factors contributing to this differential was a substantial increase in the proportion in poor blacks who were unemployed (Aguirre and
Turner, 2004). Table 2 illustrates this trend.

Table 2. Median Family Income of Blacks as a Proportion of Whites

Year	Percentages
2000	68%
1990	59%
1980	56%
1970	64%
1960	55%
1950	54%

Source: Aguirre & Turner, 2004

AFRICAN-AMERICAN POVERTY

In 2000, one out of three African Americans were poor as compared with only
one out of seven whites. African Americans were more than three times as
likely to live below the federal poverty line as white Americans. Other indicators of poverty also paint a grim picture. Some of the most blatant sources
of discrimination are present in the educational system which thus adds to
discrimination. Education, whether formal or informal is a highly valued resource and plays a major role in predicting the quality of one's life. Unfortu-
nately, African Americans suffer from limited access to education.

Given the role that neighborhoods play in access to education, residential segregation of African Americans irrespective of class further margin-
alizes African American's access to a quality education. According to Douglas Massey and Nancy Denton (1993:1), the "Spatial isolation of blacks
was achieved through racist attitudes, private behaviors and institutional
practices that disenfranchised blacks from urban housing markets and led
to the creation of ghettos." What they also discovered was the fact that
black segregation did not vary by economic class. As they reported, blacks,
no matter what their income, remained very highly segregated. The segregation index for Chicago was 91 for the poorest blacks and 86 for the most
affluent blacks. The implication is that such housing segregation has a direct impact on available financial resources for schools, leading to poor

and inferior quality education for blacks in general. One essential indicator, high school graduation rates, shows that both male and female, African Americans were far less likely to have a high school diploma (Aguirre and Turner, 2004). See Table 3.

Table 3. Educational Attainment of African Americans and Whites, (1994–2000)

Year	High School		College	
	Blacks	*Whites*	*Blacks*	*Whites*
2000	79%	80	17	28
1998	76	87	19	27
1994	73	82	13	23

Source: Aguirre and Turner,2001.

One study concluded that the observed income disparities between whites and African Americans are the result of three forces: non-labor market discrimination, past labor market discrimination, and present labor market discrimination (Schiller, 1998). Studies show that the over-representation of African Americans in poverty is directly related to the racial discrimination pervasive through American society. (Krieger and Bassett,1986; Lewin, 1991; Williams et al, 1997; Rothman, 1993; As Schiller notes, "Racial and cultural theories cannot explain all the inequities [but] racial discrimination must be held accountable (Schiller, 2004:5).

Studies have shown that poverty, especially for African Americans, results from forces beyond the control of the individual (Schiller, 2004). In other words, poverty results from restricted opportunities. As Schiller asserts, "The poor are poor because they do not have adequate access to good schools, jobs, and income " (Schiller, 2004:6). Schiller goes on to say that "In the face of these socially imposed constraints, no amount of work ethic or effort assures escape from poverty" (Schiller, 2004:6). The U.S Bureau of Census also found that the chances of escaping poverty are not equally distributed at all (U.S Bureau of the Census, 2001). African Americans had a much harder time of escaping poverty than white Americans.

SEGREGATION OF AFRICAN AMERICANS: POVERTY AND HEALTH CONSEQUENCES

There are many consequences of living in poverty, but the most serious outcome of poverty is hunger. Lack of food or access to adequate food lead to malnutrition and ill health (Physician Task Force, 1985). The impact of malnutrition depends on one's gender, age, and race. The report by the Physician Task Force states that:

> Infants of poor mothers die more frequently. They are at greater risk of low birth-weight and later health impairment. As a group, poor children are less likely to be adequately nourished and more likely to suffer growth failure than their better off peers. Poor children are at greater risk of death from malnutrition, including marasmus and kwashiorkor. Low income adults are at greater risk of certain nutrition related diseases and face significantly greater likelihood of dying at relatively early ages than other Americans (p.129).

Federal and state cuts in programs such as food stamps, federal nutrition programs have significantly worsened the health status of the poor. With only half of the household in America who are considered to be below the poverty line receiving food stamps, those fortunate enough to receive food stamps, still do not have enough to feed their families a well-balanced, nutritious meal (Hunger in America, 1985).

Indeed, as stated earlier on, racial discrimination is pervasive throughout our educational system and thus provides white students with a better education and thus better opportunities than African American children (Schiller, 2004). Assuming that African and white American children enter the educational system with equal potential, then how is it that:

1. At nine years of age, African-American students are 25 percent behind white students in reading, science and math test scores.
2. Ninety two percent of white seventeen-year olds are functionally literate compared to only fifty-eight percent of African American seventeen-year olds. (U.S. Congressional Budget Office, 1991).
3. Ninety percent of white students graduate from high school but only eighty percent of African Americans graduate (Aguirre & Turner, 2004).

Clearly, discrimination in housing and in the educational system have devastating effects (Schiller, 2004). African Americans have been found to have higher rates of unemployment and underemployment than whites. Furthermore, African Americans are far more likely than their white peers to be exposed to occupational hazards and carcinogens, even after controlling for type of job and education (Krieger,1990).

But studies analyzing the current economic picture of African Americans find that although there has been some economic progress for certain segments of the African American population, significant African American economic inequities persist, and progress has slowed or has even retreated in some respects in the last decade (Williams & Jaynes, 1989). These studies suggest that poverty results from institutional discrimination. This discrimination begins early in childhood, in school, where African American children have poorer teachers and fewer resources. As the child grows, the quality of schools that African Americans attend often becomes worse. Although high school dropout rates for African Americans far exceed those for white American, even those African Americans who do receive a high school diploma do not have the same educational, job, and/or life skills as white Americans.

Each of these relationships through a series of multiplying effects on each other has a devastating effect on the health and health care of the African American population.

Chapter Two

Health Care Disparities in the United States: A Special Problem for African Americans

Health care plays a significant role in the health status of both individuals and populations. As Levine et al. (1982) argue, health status can be analyzed as a direct result of health care quality, utilization, and access. Indeed, where organized health care is available, health statistics improve. Where such care is not available, health statistics worsen (Van Horne, 1988)

In the United States however, health care is one of the primary modes by which differential socio-economic status affects the health of each segment of the population. Without an education or a decent-paying job, African Americans cannot purchase vital health care insurance, the key to gaining access to the U.S health care system. The effects of structural inequalities within U.S society (that is, the marginal position African Americans hold in the U.S. job market) can be seen in health care disparities. Without quality preventive health care, illness, disease and death take a heavy toll (Levine et al. 1982). Thus, structural inequality, in the form of educational and job discrimination and the like, will have grave effects on the health status of a population. One of the modes through which this occurs is health care.

A health care disparity indeed exists; however, it is not only due to structural inequality in such areas as education and the job market, but to direct discrimination within the U.S health care system as well. As former Secretary of Health and Human Services Louis W. Sullivan stated "There is clear, demonstrable, and undeniable evidence of discrimination and racism in our health care system." He went on to say "I am convinced that discrimination and racism do eliminate opportunities for access to health care" (Sullivan, 1991:4).

HEALTH CARE UTILIZATION BY AFRICAN-AMERICANS

When considering health care utilization, it would seem obvious that those who are sick or injured would use health services especially non-preventive services) more often than those who enjoy better health. Similarly, a population in which rates of injury, disease, and death are higher more often would be expected to have greater health care utilization (Council on Ethical and Judicial Affairs of the American Medical Association, 1990). Thus in a health care system with real racial parity in both access and quality of care, there would be a substantially higher use of health services by the average African American (Blendon et al.1989). This, however, is not the African American experience.

When we look at health care utilization, as measured by average annual number of physician contacts per person, we see that African Americans make up to 20 percent fewer visits to physician than white Americans, regardless of income. Even white Americans in poverty make significantly more physician visits than poor African Americans. Another survey found that African Americans make significantly fewer physician visits within a one-year period than do white Americans (Blendon et al. 1989). This lower rate of visits existed even when self-reported health status was taken into account. Even those who reported themselves in excellent or good health, African Americans made significantly fewer visits to physicians (Blendon et al. 1989).

According to a 1990 study, twice as many white Americans utilized the health care system for chest pain than did African Americans. The disparity actually increased with higher family income and more health insurance (Strogatz, 1990). This lower rate of health care visits is of major concern, as mentioned earlier, given the fact that the overall health status of the African American population is generally poorer than that of white Americans.

African-American children face even grimmer circumstances. African-American boys (under the age of 18) make 35 percent fewer visits to physicians than do white American boys. African-American girls fare even worse, making 40 percent fewer visits to a physician than do white American girls (U.S. Department of Health and Human Services, 1992). African-American adolescents also face dire circumstances. A study conducted by Lieu and Associates in 1993 found that African-American adolescents utilized the health care system less than their white peers (Lieu et al.1993).

The extent of prenatal care received by African-American mothers is less than that received by white American mothers. About 25 percent fewer African-America women as compared to 15 percent of white American women receive prenatal care during the first trimester. Even more telling is that African-American women are more than twice as likely as white American women to receive late or no prenatal care (U.S. Department of Health and Human Services, 1992). This has a serious and direct impact on the high infant mortality rate that the African-American population faces.

AFRICAN-AMERICANS' PORT OF ENTRY TO HEALTH CARE

A discussion concerning health care utilization would be incomplete without referral to port of entry. "Port of entry" refers to that part of a system or institution through which one gains access. In health care, it refers to the location at which an individual or group most often receives medical treatment and/or routine checkups. Common health-care ports of entry for all Americans include private physician offices, public clinics, and hospital outpatient departments (emergency rooms).

The emergency room has generally been considered a poor source of care due to such factors as long waiting times, discontinuity of care, and lack of preventive medicine (White-Means and Thornton, 1989). The medical care received in such facilities is generally considered second rate because the long waiting periods in emergency room do not enhance the quality of care received. And, the uninsured who must often travel long distances to find providers have to still wait longer once they arrive at the emergency room for care. Although this gap has decreased proportionally since 1990, twice as many African Americans still visit emergency rooms almost twice as often per year as much as white Americans. In addition, African Americans visit a private doctor's office 20 percent less than do white Americans (U.S. Department of Health and Human Services,1992).

QUALITY OF AFRICAN AMERICAN HEALTH

The quality of care received in the emergency room by African Americans has been poorer than that received by White Americans, regardless of income. This inequality in the quality of care is due to the direct racial discrimination within the U.S. health care system (Blendon et al. 1989). For example, African Americans have been subjected to longer waiting times than white Americans ,even those African Americans who are insured are forced to wait longer than uninsured white Americans (Davis and Rowland, 1987). A 1989 study found that African Americans were more likely than white Americans to have had to wait for more than half an hour before seeing a physician at their last ambulatory visit (Blendon et al.1989).

African Americans also frequently experience a cruel and heartless process called "patient dumping." Patient dumping refers to the transfer of patients from a private emergency room to a crowded public hospital emergency room. Often this occurs because the patient does not have insurance and the hospital does not want to incur a financial loss. Because of African Americans' marginal position in the U.S. job market, African Americans experience more insurance problems and thus experience patient dumping more frequently than white Americans. In their study, Taira and Taira (1991) reported that about 87 percent of the patients dumped from private to public hospitals were black or Hispanic and uninsured. Such dumping means further closure of public hospitals to the poor community. Academic health centers and major teaching hospitals account for 27 percent of uncompensated care as a percentage of gross patient revenues (Commonwealth Fund Task Force on Academic Health Centers, 2001). Patient dumping subjects African Americans to much added pain, suffering, stress, and even life-threatening situations.

Another indicator of the poor quality of health care that African Americans receive is the kind of hospitals whose emergency rooms are utilized by African Americans. Although some are excellent, many of the internal medicine and ambulatory care teaching programs that are found in such teaching hospitals are poorly developed with inadequate faculty personnel and deficient resources, (Taira and Taira, 1991).

In nursing home care, African Americans receive a poorer standard of care than do white Americans and have a more difficult time gaining admission. Therefore, African Americans are only half as likely as white Americans to use nursing home facilities even after adjustment for other risk factors (Saver et al. 1993).

A strong indicator of the poor quality of care African Americans receive is the limited treatment they receive for even identical medical conditions. Several studies show that even after adjustment for health insurance and clinical status, whites are more likely than African Americans to receive coronary angiography, bypass surgery, angioplasty, chemo dialysis, intensive care for pneumonia, and kidney transplants (Aday, 1986).

In a national survey of patients discharged from hospitals with a diagnosis of anterior myocardial infarction, African-American men had a rate three-fourths that of white American men; however, African-American men were only half as likely to undergo angiography treatment for this condition and only one-third as likely to undergo bypass surgery as whites. Mortality rates suggest that the severity of illness is comparable between African and white Americans (Council on Ethical and Judicial Affairs of the American Medical Association, 1990; Goldberg et al. 1992). For example, compared to whites with the same severity of condition, African Americans are less likely to be seen by a cardiologist, to have coronary angiography performed, and to undergo coronary artery bypass surgery. These differences on health access would seem to account for the higher fatality rate and, in part, the excess mortality rate in African Americans as compared with white Americans (Lee et al. 1990).

One's race has been found to correlate negatively with the likelihood that a patient with kidney disease will receive long-term hemodialysis or a kidney transplant. Indeed, several studies have documented racial disparities among patients who undergo kidney transplantation (Kjellstand and Logan, 1987). In one study, white dialysis recipients were 33 percent more likely than African-American patients to receive kidney transplants (Kjellstand and Logan 1987).

Furthermore, racism is clearly seen in patterns of all organ donations as African Americans must wait twice as long as white Americans for their first transplant (Sullivan, 1991). A study examining the pattern of treatment for patients hospitalized because of pneumonia found that the patient's being African American correlated negatively with the intensity of care provided (Sullivan, 1991). The study showed that after controlling for difference in clinical characteristics and income, African Americans were less likely to receive appropriate medical services.

In a recent controlled experiment by Schulman et al (1999), they assessed physicians' treatment recommendation for patients presenting various types of chest pain. They hypothesized that "The race and sex of the patient would influence the physician's recommendation regarding cardiac catheterization." A random sample of 720 primary care physicians took part in the study. The study confirmed that "Patient's race and sex may influence a physician's recommendation with respect to cardiac catheterization, regardless of the patient's clinical characteristics." They concluded that "Bias or overt prejudice may [occur] when a patients' membership in a target group automatically activates a cultural stereotype in the physician's memory regardless of the level of prejudice the physician has" (625).

QUALITY OF PRENATAL CARE FOR AFRICAN AMERICANS

Not only are there gaps in the amount of prenatal care received by African American pregnant women compared with white women, but also in the quality of care they receive. For example, compared with white women, African-American women receiving prenatal care were less likely to receive advice on drinking, smoking, and general health that could have reduced the chances of these having an adverse effect on their pregnancy (Kogan et al. 1994). These issues are of great concern especially when one uncovers references to

studies such as that conducted in 1990 which found African-American
women at high risk of delivering a low-birth weight infants compared to
white women (Kogan et al.1994).

MEDICAL INSURANCE FOR AFRICAN AMERICANS

African Americans prefer private physician care just as much as other Americans do but are less likely to receive that kind of care. One of the causes of
the serious U.S. health problem is health insurance problems for African
Americans. Low health care utilization can be attributed in part to African
Americans' disproportionate lack of any insurance at all. African Americans
possess 25 percent less private insurance than whites (U.S. Department of
Health and Human Services, 1992).

As already suggested, the dominant path to insurance is through the work
place. Since African Americans are less likely to be employed and the unemployment rate is twice that of the national average, they suffer from lack of
access to health insurance. As a matter of fact, the proportion of the uninsured
among African Americans is about 22 percent. Furthermore, groups with the
highest uninsured rate are low-wage workers or workers in the secondary
markets. Since African Americans are over-represented in this sector of the
labor market, this makes them more than likely to be uninsured. As Davis
(2003:8) reported for African Americans, "The uninsured rates vary from a
low of 8 percent in five states (Rhode Island, Minnesota, Massachusetts,
Iowa, and Wisconsin) to highs of 23 percent in Texas and 22 percent in New
Mexico." Private insurance is the most widely accepted of all medical insurance plans and allows the possessor a great deal of freedom in terms of health
care accessibility (Reed, 1992). Yet African Americans are significantly less
likely to have no insurance than are white Americans over a whole year. In
1988, 85 percent of the uninsured nationally were either working or were
family members of workers (Friedman, 1991).

IMPACT ON ELDERLY AFRICAN-AMERICANS

Perhaps the most severely impoverished African-Americans are elderly. They
live on fixed incomes. Many have been forced into early retirement by their
work skills becoming redundant (Schiller, 1998). Many of those aged who re-
turn to work after retirement to supplement their incomes find jobs only in the
low-income secondary market. Of the aged poor, 77 percent depend on Social Security payments as their sole source of income (Schiller, 1998).

As for the aged African Americans who have some resources, for the most part, their meager dividends and investments are inadequate. For the most part these poor African Americans average only about $70,000 in assets, including a home (Schiller, 1998). But one out of every four African American approaching retirement has less than four thousand dollars net worth exclusive of their homes (Schiller, 1998). Such low liquidity has a direct impact on health care. Since Social Security income alone cannot pay for increasing medical costs, many African Americans who do have some resources must sell their homes in order to qualify for Medicaid.

But research demonstrates that enrollment in Medicaid does not eliminate all the problems of access to health care. In fact, while Medicaid may reduce the cost barriers to health care, such non-economic barriers as racism, discrimination, and particular health care system characteristics still impede African Americans' access to health care services. For example, until recently, some states did not provide Medicaid coverage for the first trimester of pregnancy, when prenatal care is most essential. Moreover, Medicaid does not guarantee either continuity of care or high-quality health care as we shall see later.

MEDICAID

Federally funded health care programs have contributed to improvements in the health and well-being of those they serve, including African Americans, who have thereby gained access to physicians and other health services. Poor African Americans with health coverage make twice as many visits to physicians as those without health coverage.

Therefore, while Medicaid has provided the entry point through which many poor African Americans can gain health care, the extent to which services are fully available to them and others is often minimal. Indeed, only one-third of all Medicaid beneficiaries, or 6.6 million individuals were African Americans (Davis and Rowland, 1987). In other words, Medicaid covers only about one-half of the 12 million poor African Americans with incomes below the poverty level.

Another disturbing trend with Medicaid is that the now ended families receiving Aid to Families with Dependent Children (AFDC) made up 70 to 75 percent of the Medicaid population, three-fourths of Medicaid expenses actually were solely for the costs of care for the aged, blind, and otherwise disabled, especially patients in nursing homes (McKenzie,1994). This has persisted even under the 1996 Personal Responsibility and Work Opportunity Reconciliation Act.

Previous research on the effects of Medicaid on the utilization of pediatric care among all low-income American children suggests that Medicaid improves children's access to health care, but simultaneously reduces access to office-based physicians (Rosenbach, 1989). That is, after Medicaid went into effect, patients with children went from securing health care in a physician's office to getting it at a clinic or health center. At the same time, Medicaid children still have a higher probability of visiting an office-based physician than have low income privately insured or uninsured children. But the insured, whether through Medicaid or private insurance fare much better than the uninsured in obtaining hospital services. Furthermore the insured make more efficient use of hospitals. Indeed, in general, low-income Americans average more hospital admissions and physician visits than those with higher incomes simply because of their overall poorer health status.

Medicaid coverage is also affected by the discontinuity of physician care. African Americans are still less likely than whites to see one particular physician for care. Seventy-eight percent of whites, compared to 68 percent of African Americans have a regular family physician (Aday, 1986). And, as already noted, there has also been a decrease in African Americans' use of the doctor's office as a port of entry into the health system, and a corresponding shift to such other entry points as government clinics, hospital outpatient departments, or emergency rooms. These providers are less likely to offer clients any physician continuity. The majority of health-care seekers in these ports of entry are African Americans. Of course, this shift from private physicians to more public forms of regular care is a direct result of cost-cutting financial pressures that ultimately serve to limit health care for the poor.

As part of the federal government's attempt to control health care costs, the Omnibus Budget and Reconciliation Act of 1981 (OBRA) drastically reduced the federal share of Medicaid spending. The OBRA budget gave states greater flexibility over the design of their Medicaid programs. States were given greater autonomy in setting standard requirements for eligibility and need. As a result, many states do not currently extend coverage to two-parent families or to medically needy individuals who are impoverished by large medical expenses (Davis et al. 1990). Further, most states restricted the use of required and optional benefits by limiting the number of physician visits. Many states now require hospitals and doctors to get prior authorization from state regulators before certain surgeries and other procedures are performed. From the Joint Commission on Accreditation of Health Care Organization (JCAHO) and Medicare have come requirements for hospitals to institute utilization reviews to ensure the necessity and appropriateness of each post-surgical physician care plans. The introduction of the Diagnosis Related Groups (DRGs)—A patient classification scheme which provides a means of relating the types of patients a hospital treats to the costs incurred by the hospital by classifying patients based on diagnosis—originated from the Medicare cost containment program of 1983 (Fetter, 1991). The establishment of Peer Review Organizations (PROs) have had a major negative impact on how physicians and hospital administrators service patients, especially those on Medicaid (Davis et al. 1990).

Yet, despite such changes in port of entry, Medicaid coverage has not expanded for the poor as we shall see. But Medicaid personnel in public facilities have been providing for the poor a greater portion of care.

Private hospitals have not expanded their services to the poor. In fact, since 1980, African Americans have experienced decreased medical attention as a result of federal cutbacks. To the extent that private physicians and private hospitals have been involved at all, they have received generous financial incentives from Medicaid (Temkin-Greener and Clark, 1988).

Hospitalization records show that the poor in general, and African Americans in particular, have higher rates of hospitalization than higher-income groups (Aday, 1986). But such hospitalization rates, of course, do not translate into increased access to health care generally or of course, high-quality health care. Instead, such high hospitalization rates reflect not only the poorer health status of African Americans, but also the inefficient and inadequately organized U.S. health care system, and increased privatization of other public services leading to systematic exclusion of the poor.

In fact a central factor in lower quality care for the poor is private physicians non-participation in Medicaid services. Overall, approximately 35 percent of all private physicians have not accepted Medicaid, including 37 percent of obstetricians and gynecologists. Forty percent of cardiologists and psychiatrists have not accepted Medicaid patients (Davis et al. 1990). Participation by such physicians in the Medicaid system could reduce the high infant mortality rates of African Americans and the high mortality rates from heart disease and injuries (Davis et al.1990). Access to physicians with specialized knowledge and training may be especially critical for African Americans whose low socio-economic status has already placed them at higher risk of illness. But even if there were increased availability of health services through Medicaid insurance, there would still be several factors inhibiting African Americans' access to and use of adequate health services. Many poor are ineligible for Medicaid in various states even when their income is well below the poverty line. Between 1980 and 2000, the U.S. population without health insurance increased by more than a third, from approximately twenty-eight to forty-four million (Kuttner, 1999). And African Americans are the least likely Americans to be insured.

As has been demonstrated in this discussion, two issues impact negatively on African American health; poverty and lack of insurance. The current U.S.

health care system based on a combination of private insurance and public programs with strict eligibility requirements (age, income, health and family status) has not solved the problem of access (OECD, 1992).

At any given time, about 15 percent of those under 65 years of age and 13 percent of the entire American population have no health insurance. Because 62 percent of health insurance provision is employment-based, African Americans with weak connections to the labor market have a high probability of being uninsured (Friedman, 1995).

STRESS

Stress is defined as a "heightened mind-body reaction to stimuli inducing fear or anxiety in the individual." (Cockerham, 2004:62). Stress occurs in response to strainful and threatening situations in the environment. For African Americans, coping with every day racism and increased impoverishment, poverty affect their susceptibility to certain diseases caused by their unique situation in America.

Poverty affect the health status of African Americans through the stress caused by their marginal status in American society. The stress comes from living in depressed inner-city neighborhoods, struggling to pay the bills, exposure to frequent community violence, feelings of powerlessness and hopelessness, confronting institutional discrimination on a regular basis, and frequent family disruptions that many African Americans experience daily from birth to death (LaVeist, 1992).

The term "endemic stress" emphasizes long-term, continuing burdens, such as constant exposure to violence and prolonged unemployment, and their health consequences for African Americans who have to cope with them daily (Miller, 1987). A study by Susser, Watson and Hopper (1985) similarly found that African Americans, because of their poverty, experience economic hardships, frustrated aspirations, chronic insecurity about jobs, and frequent disruption of social ties (Susser, Watson and Hopper, 1985). A study by LaVeist, (1993) found that African Americans, because of racial discrimination, had diminished self-esteem, feelings of loss, and a learned hopelessness.

According to Miller (1987:6), "The experiences of poverty and inequality and uncertainty about how one is perceived because of one's race is certainly a type of continuing, prolonged stress for African Americans." He went on to say that such stress not only makes its victims susceptible to social distress but also susceptible to acute illnesses. Internalized racism by African Americans leads to lower levels of happiness and life satisfaction and higher levels of chronic health problems and psychological distress (Williams, 1996).

Some researchers have sought to understand the role of this "endemic stress" on the lives of even affluent African Americans. They found that successful African Americans cite the limitations on their occupational progress and their stressful encounters on the job (Manton, Patrick, and Johnson, 1987). Recent research indicates that exposure to community violence has adverse health effects through stress (Williams, 1996). The combination of living in physically dangerous urban areas and the maintenance of constant psychological vigil and for dealing with the assaults of racial bias, that African Americans frequently face can adversely affect their health status. Three studies using blood pressure measurement procedures have found that, compared with whites, African Americans have higher blood pressures during sleep. This suggests that African Americans' perceived need to cope actively with their environment may lead them to unconsciously maintain a higher level of physiological arousal even at night (Krieger,1990).

Such daily turmoil and stress in the lives of African Americans is immense. This stress can lead to a number of health problems, including hypertension.

HYPERTENSION AND DIABETES IN AFRICAN AMERICANS

In the diagnosis and treatment of hypertension and diabetes, which account for a majority of the illness, morbidity, and mortality rates among African Americans, the results of prejudice and discrimination are common. The African American hypertensive and diabetic is more likely than white counterparts to die from these ailments and to have strokes, end-stage renal disease, and heart failure. These complications are a direct result of the inaccessibility of proper treatment, delay in diagnosis and treatment, and inability to get adequate and appropriate pharmacological treatment.

In the United States, more diabetic and hypertensive patients visit physicians for treatment due to the nature of their illness than for any other medical disorder. Through improvements in health-related programs, the number of deaths from stroke, kidney disease, and coronary disease have declined over the years. However, among African Americans these successes have been less striking. Accounting for this disparity are racial differences in availability of health care services. Disparities in health care for diagnosis and treatment still persist to the detriment of the African-American population.

Arterial hypertension is defined as elevated arterial blood pressure (BP). Essential or primary hypertension is arterial hypertension of unknown cause. Patients with essential hypertension have an exaggerated response to stress and an exaggerated response to relaxation. More than 60 million peoples in the United States have hypertension.

Numerous epidemiological studies have demonstrated not only the higher prevalence of hypertension among the African American community but also their excess morbidity and mortality from it. Data from the Joint National Report of the Committee on Detection, Evaluation, and Treatment of High Blood Pressure have shown the discrepancies in prevalence, incidence and complications among African Americans, Latinos and whites in this country. The prevalence of hypertension is higher among African Americans than whites. Although the reasons for its higher prevalence among African-Americans are not altogether determined, this has been attributed to African American's genetic heredity, higher salt intake, and greater environmental stress (Wright, 1988).

Studies show that African Americans are likely to develop hypertension at an earlier age than whites (Wright, 1988). Approximately twenty-five percent of the African American population has been diagnosed with uncontrolled or essential hypertension; the number of patients with essential hypertension account for 95 percent of all hypertensive patients. More patients visit physicians for hypertension than for any other disorder. Yet, there is still a substantial increase in cardiovascular diseases among African Americans, resulting, in part, from hypertension that was never detected, let alone treated. Indeed, the differences can be attributed, in part, to the failure of national health programs to provide sufficient health education for African Americans about hypertension. As a result, more whites than African Americans are aware of their hypertensive state, receiving proper treatment, and controlling their condition. The issue of health education is as much a part of access to health care as treatment. Survival rates for those with acute ischemic attacks are directly related to early detection and treatment of the process in the appropriate health care setting (Tierney,1990). In this sense, access to health care can also be defined in terms of availability and quality of the health care facilities, accompanied by the attitudinal and socioeconomic factors that limit or encourage the use of such facilities.

Psychological factors have also been implicated in the higher prevalence of hypertension in the African American population. According to James et al. (1987), the prevalence of hypertension is negatively correlated with greater education and income, and showed a positive association with an index of frustration called "John Henryism." This has been labeled as a key behavioral factor in the development of hypertension among African Americans.

The concept of "John Henryism" refers to a strong personality predisposed to engaging in active coping strategies against social stressors. At high levels of "John Henryism," its inverse association with socioeconomic status should be stronger than at low "John Henryism." In their most recent study, James et al (1987) found a significantly higher percentage of hypertension among

African Americans classified as exhibiting high John Henryism/low socio-economic status than in any of the other John Henryism/socio-economic groups. That is, at the higher levels of John Henryism, African Americans in the low socio-economic groups were three times as likely to be hypertensive as African Americans in the higher socio-economic groups.

According to the researchers, John Henryism as a score, in and of itself, does not increase risk for hypertension. Rather, the results indicate that such risk increases only when a high score is combined with inadequate coping resources, as might be signified by low formal education, unskilled and low-paying jobs, or abject poverty. The correlation between social stress and hypertension is one that is only now being examined as a potential, and indeed significant, factor in the epidemiology of hypertension.

Additional contributors to the high rate of hypertension in African Americans, as indicated by the research, include suppressed hostility. Krieger and Bassett (1986) concluded from their research that a tendency to hold anger in when provoked was associated with higher blood pressure, and a greater prevalence of documented hypertension compared with those who reported an overt-anger coping style.

Moreover, the lower the education level achieved, the more likely a subject was to be diagnosed as hypertensive. However, although controlling for education level reduced the discrepancy between African Americans and whites in hypertension, African Americans at the highest educational level were still twice as likely as whites to be diagnosed as hypertensive. Thus educational level is not directly correlated with increased chance of hypertension. Rather, race, as a social phenomenon, plays a role. Other potential contributors include social stress from the environment, lack of social support, urban-rural residence and stressful family interaction patterns. Endemic stress is thus another mode by which poverty and discrimination affect the health status of African Americans.

DIABETES

The effect of economic barriers in the care of diabetic African-American patients is increasingly seen as important in its diagnosis and treatment. Studies conducted by the National Medical Care Expenditure Survey (1988) concluded that people with diabetes often have difficulty obtaining individual health insurance at an affordable price and may not find employment providing adequate medical coverage. Insurance companies may offer only limited coverage to diabetics or charge higher premiums because of the nature of the illness and the severe complications of end stage renal disease which often

occur. Levels of hospital reimbursement for outpatient care and medical sup-
plies affects the quality of care that diabetics receive, since these differ by
type of coverage, state of residence, and the Medicaid procedure being used.

In this chapter, a careful review of the sociological literature on health and
illness, as it relates to African-American health status demonstrates the importance of race, class, and institutional patterns of discrimination as important variables influencing access to health by African Americans.

ENVIRONMENTAL FACTORS
IN AFRICAN-AMERICAN HEALTH

As alluded to earlier on, the low health care status of many poor Americans
can be attributed partly to the environment in which they live. These are
mostly urban areas in which African Americans constitute 59% of the population (LaVeist, 1993). Thirty percent of urban African Americans live in areas of concentrated poverty. These areas are often referred to as "ghettos"
(Warren, 1995). These are unpleasant and unsafe places to live. Middle class
African Americans who could afford to live elsewhere nevertheless also still
experience residential segregation because of prejudice and discrimination.
Those who do manage to leave, leave the ghettos with fewer role models and
even more limited financial resources (Anderson, 1990). The exodus from the
poor neighborhoods creates heightened problems and instability. As a result
of institutional and individual discrimination in the housing market, middle
and working class African Americans cannot go far in their quest for a decent
environment (Baugh,1991). Thus, residential segregation forces a large frac-
tion of the African American middle class to live on the rim of the African
American community, in situations not much better to those of whites
(Lewin, 1991).

Urban ghettos are characterized by concentrated unemployment. This
unemployment further perpetuates poverty. High levels of unemployment,
create a social environment in which people are isolated from the labor
market. African Americans growing up in a neighborhood of concentrated
unemployment are less likely to know someone who is employed, which
lowers the employability options of individuals in the area because personal ties and friendship connections are among the most important methods for gaining jobs and relatively few jobs are found by responding to ads
or just talking to employers.

Furthermore, since a smaller proportion of these are employed, there
are fewer people to serve as models from which others can learn about the

process of job search which further alienates the ghetto residents from the labor market (Anderson, 1990). The United States concentrated unemployment within a ghetto causes further unemployment, leading to a snowballing effect of poverty (Massey & Shibuya, 1995), since less than half of African American men of working age are part of the labor force (Steinberg, 1989).

Most poor health, including mortality rates is directly linked to the environment. Roux et al. (2001:99) examined the "relation between characteristics of neighborhoods and the incidence of coronary heart disease." They found that residents of disadvantaged neighborhoods-those that had more unfavorable risk-factor profiles—had a higher risk of disease than residents of advantaged neighborhoods, even when controlled for personal income, education, and occupation.

Children in poor communities are subject to street killings, dangerous housing, drugs and alcohol, as well as physical and mental abuse (Jackson, 1993) The influence of these factors upon the future life of these children is immense. Although children growing up in ghettos may not at first exhibit behavior typical of the inner city, they eventually display lower levels of academic achievement, crime, drug abuse, and teenage childbearing are observed (Mincy, 1989).

The presence of excess amounts of pollutants and toxic chemicals in inner cities further compromises the health of African Americans. Air pollution in African-American ghettos is higher than in white suburbs. Poor African Americans living in the inner city are likely to be exposed to lead poisoning, radioactivity, tobacco use, air pollution and can cause growth retardation in children and affect their weight and height. Children growing up under such conditions are more likely to have birth defects or other health issues, and to have children of their own with such problems.

CONCLUSION

In summary, the United States health care system, as it is currently constituted, does not provide an equal distribution of health resources across all ethnic and social classes. The poorest and "darkest" are those who are least served by the U.S. health system.

The rise in the 1990s of the number of African Americans who are in poverty places them in a particularly precarious position within the health care system. In explaining access to health care by African Americans, the National Health Interview Survey (1990:2) stated that, "Differences in survival and health are not solely explained by poverty, but by unique experiences and cultural orientations of African Americans." Much more ethnographic research is needed on how perceptions of health, and other attitudes and beliefs impact on the choice of care by African Americans. To examine these issues, I explored health-seeking behavior, attitudes, and experiences of selected African Americans in Boston, Massachusetts and the city of Schenectady in upstate New York.

Chapter Three

African-American
Health-Seeking Behavior

This chapter focuses on health-seeking behavior among African Americans in two communities in the northeastern United States. The general aim was to assess the health status of African Americans. This research was conducted in June 1991 and August 1992 in the predominantly African-American Boston area communities of Dorchester, Roxbury, and Mattapan.

In formulating the research questions, several earlier studies of African-American health were examined which suggested a number of research trajectories. To address central questions about African-American health, the study developed an interview schedule (See Appendix A) to investigate African-American attitudes, beliefs, and perceptions relating to health and to health care delivery systems. In the interview schedule, some of the conversations lasted from an hour to one and a half hours.

METHODOLOGY

To obtain a fairly representative sample of African Americans in the various Boston communities, six settings were chosen. Three of those settings were people's homes in Government assisted housing (projects) and two were in areas identified as residential neighborhoods for middle to lower-income African Americans. I also chose five non-residential settings which could be described as attracting working class African Americans. These settings were selected after a careful review of census tract information on the area. In a nutshell, the sample came from two federal housing (projects), two barber shops frequented by lower to middle class African Americans, a tropical-food market, a laundro-mat, and a bus station in downtown Roxbury-Dorchester.

Eighty-five African Americans were interviewed. The focus of the interview was to find out what they saw as the causes of illness, informants' knowledge about health services utilization options and constraints and the beliefs about the bases for health in general and their use of folk medicine in particular. Finally the interview explored what is it that influences African Americans' choice of health therapies. There responses were transcribed and content analysis were performed on the interview transcripts. Questions were asked to elicit whether traditional African culture (beliefs in the power of ancestors and in the efficacy of folk medicine) influenced their utilization of "formal" versus "informal" health systems.

FINDINGS

From the study (37%) thirty-seven percent of respondents believed that sickness is caused by people not taking care of themselves. A few more respondents listed, "poor hygiene" "poor nutrition" and "drug abuse" as habits which lead to illness. About 8 percent considered sickness to be caused by exposure to the environments in the sense of "change of weather" or "viruses." It is sufficiently clear that unlike Africans and their beliefs about the causes of sickness, this evidence on African-American beliefs shows that disproportional use of the health care system is not due to a belief that sickness is a form of punishment, a prevalent view among traditional African communities (Bonsi, 1972: Bailey,1991). But also important in the findings from this research is that although 37 percent of respondents recognized that not taking care of oneself can cause illness, 63 percent of all the respondents did not draw any connections between preventive care and good health. The evidence does seem to point on the whole to these African Americans having a reasonable well-grounded knowledge of issues about health and what makes one unhealthy or sick.

As for low utilization of health services, more than half mentioned that socio-economic status, prejudice and discrimination determines one's access to health care. Nevertheless, about 78 percent of those interviewed believed in other forces rather than "scientific" medicine as healing tools. Most significantly, 60 percent of those who believed in the power of other forces identified prayer specifically as a healing tool. This does not, however, suggest that prayer is their only method of treating illness. Another significant observation was that although prayer is a powerful form of healing, 55 percent of the praying sample stated that they would seek and had sought formal medical help as well. They explained this apparent paradox by asserting that physicians derive their knowledge and expertise from God and that when the religious respondents see a physician, they do so because physicians are working on behalf of God. Thus, any healing process for them includes this religious element.

Of the 44 percent who received Medicaid and or Medicare, 9 percent had not seen a health care practitioner at all during the previous two years. The rest (91%) reported seeing a health care provider at least once within the last three years. All those who could afford their own health insurance, or had jobs which provided insurance coverage reported more frequent visits to the health care providers. These results confirm earlier studies by Davis et al (1990) that if health care treatment is affordable, increased utilization of health care services will result. Consistent with previous research (Jones & Rice,1988), those who paid their own bills independent of public assistance or using private insurance reported mostly positive encounters with health care providers. A couple of the respondents commented, however, that if they did not have the money they would have received poor service.

Indicating under what conditions these individuals chose not to use the health care services when they were sick, most reported that medical attention was not sought because the nature of the ailment was not severe enough to require hospital care. This probably indicates a lack of awareness about access to other options and levels of health care services, apart from the hospital setting. It could also be inferred from their responses that they believe that only serious problems require immediate medical attention. This might not be as positive as it sounds because it may mean that they do not seek treatment early enough. In fact, their common reference to hospitals as the source of medical attention indicates that the main port of entry for African Americans is the emergency room (See White-Means and Thornton, 1989).

SCHENECTADY, NEW YORK

To replicate these findings, a similar study exploring the health experiences and perceptions of African Americans was undertaken in Schenectady New York. The objective was to examine whether traditional health beliefs and practices of African Americans as reported in the sociological literature were consistent with those of a target population of low-income African Americans in Schenectady County of New York.

SETTING

Schenectady County in 2003 City Census comprised of 143,439 Whites (95.7%), 4,682 African-Americans (3.1%), and 1,825 (1.2%) of other ethnic groups including Eskimos, Aleuts, Asians, Pacific Islanders, American Indians and people from Spanish-language countries (Latinos). In Schenectady County, these populations are residentially fairly well segregated from one another. Most African-Americans and Latinos live within the city of Schenectady and tend to be highly concentrated in the neighborhoods of Hamilton Hill and Central State Street. (See Diagram I).

METHODOLOGY

The data were obtained from questionnaire survey and in-depth interviews with low-income African Americans who were receiving medical services at community-based clinics in the poorest section of Schenectady, a small rust-belt city in upstate New York. Its neighborhood has the highest proportion of African-Americans in the city. This clinic provided an appropriate setting for reaching the research objectives, as approximately one-third of the patients were African American.

Only African-American clients were given the questionnaire. Questions focused on the role of beliefs and attitudes in their choice of treatment, the regularity of their health care use, the influence of their religious beliefs, and their illness experiences and medical care. The survey was answered anonymously, in the waiting room usually by the participant. However, when the patient was not able to read because of poor eye sight, or illiteracy, or did not feel like completing the questionnaire, the questions were read aloud and their responses recorded.

Questions were designed to address the central questions about African-Americans' health and their beliefs and perceptions relating to health and health care delivery systems, was conducted in the geographical areas mentioned. To obtain a representative sample of African Americans, subjects were randomly selected by sight in the waiting room with no specific regard to occupation, age and gender. Out of the 70 questionnaires made available for distribution, fifty-one African Americans of different socio-economic backgrounds were contacted. This was conducted from April to December in 1994. Out of the 70, 8 refused,12 were not fully completed. They were therefore excluded from the rest of the analyses.

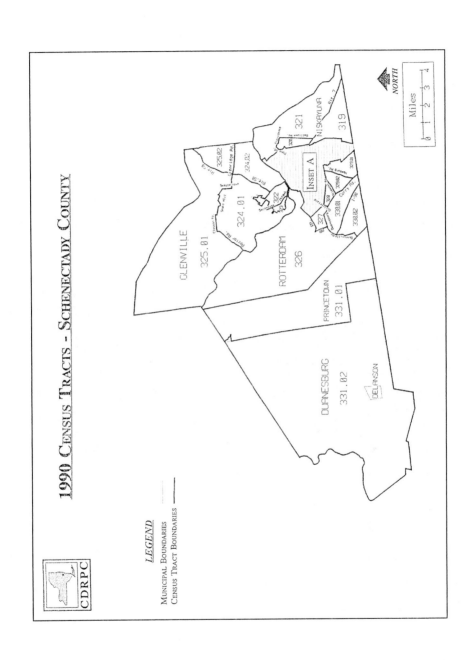

1990 Census Tracts - Schenectady County

LEGEND

Municipal Boundaries ....
Census Tract Boundaries ————

CDRPC

GLENVILLE
325.01

325.02

324.02

324.01

ROTTERDAM
326

322

NISKAYUNA
319

321

INSET A

327

330.01

330.02

PRINCETOWN
331.01

DUANESBURG
331.02

DELANSON

NORTH

Miles
0 1 2 3 4

Relatively little is known about the medical beliefs of urban African Americans and their health-seeking behaviors. Although, according to Watson (1984) and Snow (1978), popular definitions of good health for urban and rural African Americans include taking responsibility for one's health, while being able to live independently and meeting one's daily needs are aspects of African American health-seeking behavior. The research explored the following:

1. The effects of African Americans' beliefs and attitudes about health and health care on how African Americans choose health treatment;
2. The degree of regularity in African Americans use of health resources;
3. The relationships of African Americans economic background, religious affiliation, and gender to health care utilization;
4. Whether African Americans experience with health care and health care professionals has been such as to encourage or discourage their seeking medical help when sick.

The semi-structured interviews consisted of twenty-six questions, asking for a wide range of information, including gender, age, financial status, educational level and religious affiliations, as well as more in-depth questions, including health complaints and belief in faith and prayer as healing tools. *See Appendix A for survey schedule)

In *Doing Field Research* Johnson (1975:4) states that "There is a critical relationship between the initial entry to a setting and the validity of the data subsequently collected." Therefore I worked to establish trust and respect between myself and each participant. To accomplish that, I decided at first that a "professional" approach would be more appropriate and work better by lending more credibility to what I was doing and allowing the participants to feel the importance of their contribution. I wore a shirt and tie and suit pants slacks, shoes and assumed a very formal demeanor. But this proved unsuccessful, so I chose a middle-of-the road strategy, taking a more personal, relaxed stance and wearing a T-shirt and khaki slacks. The participants were more at ease and in the initial casual conversations that we had, they seemed much more willing to provide me with answers.

To develop a sense of trust it was important to appear interested and empathetic. Surprising many research subjects would even contribute more information simply because they were lonely or bored waiting to schedule an appointment or to see a health care provider.

The data were first coded by analyzing the demographic profile of respondents and identifying major themes from the data. To overcome ambiguities in words and phrases, a content analysis was also performed and the emerging themes were coded as well.

DATA ANALYSIS

Of the fifty-one participants at the Health Center, almost three-fourths (73 percent) were female, while 28 percent were males. Of the sample, 54 percent were unemployed. Eighteen percent had received less than ten years of schooling. Seventy-eight percent of these respondents labeled themselves as religious and eighty percent considered faith and prayer as effective healing tools. Table 4 summarizes the demographic characteristics of respondents.

Table 4. Demographics of African-American Health Clinic Respondents (N = 51)

Demographic Profile	N	Percent
Sex		
Male	14	28
Female	37	72
Total	51	100%
Age		
20–25	7	14
26–31	10	20
32–36	10	19
37+	24	47
Total	51	100%
Occupation and Income Source		
Blue collar	13	26
White collar	7	14
Unemployed,	6	12
Employed & Public Assistance	4	8
Unemployed but on		
Public Assistance	21	40
Total	51	100
Education		
High School	22	43
Less than high school	8	18
More than high school	20	39
Total	51	100%

• Distributions do not always total 100% due to rounding.

FINDINGS

The study concluded that respondent's decisions concerning health care and the choice of treatment were closely connected to their religious beliefs. Yet, despite the significant role that religion plays in these people's conception of health and utilization of health care, seventy-five percent of the African American population surveyed still sees a doctor first when ill.

Respondents were asked to evaluate and comment on their experiences of care received from health care providers. Eighty-seven percent reported that they felt comfortable with the care they received at the clinic. Clearly, these African Americans are not kept away from organized medicine by their strong belief in faith and prayer as healing tools.

Contrary to other research findings about low utilization of health services by African Americans compared with whites (McDonald et al. 1988), we found that 78 percent of those at the Health Center surveyed reported visiting a doctor more than twice a year and twenty-seven percent more than four times a year. The frequency of their visits leads us to believe that this clinic and its clients are not typical. After all this Health Center is at the heart of Hamilton Hill. The proximity of the clinic to poor working African Americans, the good rapport observed between the staff and the patients, as well as the clinic's acceptance of Medicaid and Medicare makes it more accessible to the African-American community than a great many health care facilities.

A question on the use of health care services was designed to measure whether African Americans' experience with health care professionals or other health care providers discourages them from seeking medical help when needed.

However, the connection between social class and health care utilization at the Center is clear at least in some respects. The more money one has (as determined by the type of job), the better the insurance one has and the better the services. Those with limited incomes or the unemployed were far less likely to seek medical care at a doctor's office as reported by the respondents.

Among the unemployed, 81% used the clinic as their primary access to health care, while only 43% of white-collar workers did so. Those covered by private or federal insurance or by jobs that provided insurance coverage consulted medical practitioners on a regular basis. The results confirm earlier findings that if health care treatment is affordable, the utilization of health care services will increase (Saver and Peterfreud, 1993; Davis et al. 1991). Consistent with other research results (Davis et al. 1991) those who paid their own bills independent of public assistance or had private insurance reported most positive encounters with the care they received.

Some respondents commented, however, that if they had not had money they would have received poor service. This suggests that these respondents may have known of poor people who had been poorly treated. This not withstanding, about half of the respondents who were Medicaid and Medicare beneficiaries reported positive experiences with health care providers compared to the rest of the sample.

But slightly over a third of the Medicaid and Medicare recipients had had negative experiences with health care providers. The respondents reported that they had to "wait too long to schedule appointments," "had appointments pushed back," or had to "wait longer than everyone else at the time of their appointment." This is consistent with research that shows that Medicaid and Medicare recipients having a hard time finding and getting quality care (Friedman, 1995).

To determine the extent to which such experiences might influence future utilization of health care services, it was necessary to determine under what circumstances these individuals had chosen not to seek health care services when they were sick. The findings were consistent with the Boston study (about 50%) since eighty-six percent surveyed at the Center replied that they did not seek medical attention when they felt the ailment was not thought serious enough to require hospital care.

An attempt was made to examine the extent to which cultural factors influence the choice of health care utilization among these African Americans. The results showed the influence of values on health-seeking behavior among African Americans. The questions offer insight into the extent of the impact of cultural factors, quite aside from socio-economic and racial barriers, on African Americans in need of health care. It can also be inferred from the study that the reality of African-American marginality to the economy, as well as specific acts of racism and discrimination, are more important determinants of these African Americans' health.

Economic factors are shown to be highly important for these respondents' use of formal health care since those who receive government assistance in financing their health care receive less adequate care than those who can afford to pay for their own health care. The overwhelming majority of people who responded that they had good relations with the health care delivery system were in a position to pay for health services by means other than Medicaid or Medicare.

Of those receiving aid, about half reported their experiences with the health care practitioners as poor and inadequate. Obviously, receiving less than adequate care because of financial limitations could effectively limit the choice to use the health care system except in the case of dire emergency.

The effect of this can be seen in the use of emergency rooms as ports of entry for health care for African Americans. On the national average, about 20% of African Americans use the emergency room as their single port of entry into the health care system (Quaye, 1994). As mentioned earlier, African Americans health status differentials are affected by life opportunities and conditions than by the medical care itself. As eloquently described by Fried-man, employment status play an important role of having health insurance for all or part of a year (Friedman, 1991). As we have seen because of racial discrimination in the labor market, African Americans are more likely to be unemployed and uninsured than whites. Consequently, African Americans have far less access to the wealth necessary to purchase health insurance and health service. African Americans are more concentrated than whites in low-paying jobs in the secondary labor market. That is, the economic structure of the U.S. labor market perpetuates the position of African Americans as a source of low wage labor, guaranteeing low income for most African Americans (Schiller, 1998).

Incidents of racial discrimination's discouraging African-Americans respondents from seeking regular medical attention were reported in their survey responses. Many complained of having to wait longer than whites did for appointments and constantly having their appointment times pushed back to accommodate white people. This was reported as due to prejudice and discrimination against their race and class. This confirms several studies that have found evidence of racism in the health care access of African Americans.

The most recent investigation on this subject by Goldberg and his colleagues reported on racial and community factors as important variables influencing coronary artery by-pass surgeries (Goldberg et al, 1992).

In their investigation, they concluded that nationally the Coronary Artery Graft Bypass (CAGB) rate was 27.1 per 1000 for whites but only 7.6 for African Americans. They concluded that for patients insured by Medicare, race is strongly associated with CABG rates. In just completed study Schulman et al (1999:623) reported that the "race and sex of the patient affected the physicians' decision about whether to refer patients with chest pain for cardiac catheterization, even when they adjusted for symptoms." The study concluded that "Men and whites were significantly more likely to be referred than women and blacks." The mean referral rate for blacks was 84.7% compared with 90.6% for whites (Schulman et al.,1999). The combination of two factors being black and being poor has held back African Americans from the medical attention that they need. Adequate use of the health delivery system have been kept from African Americans.

The argument that African Americans do not use the available medical system because it is not in keeping with their beliefs only perpetuates their not being offered quality health care. Thus, the rise in the number of African Americans in poverty demonstrates the precarious nature of class and race in the health of African Americans.

Federal government intervention in the area of urban health is severely limited. All that the urban poor have for health care coverage are overburdened and unresponsive Medicaid and Medicare systems. Federal cutbacks in recent years have further disadvantaged those African Americans who do receive Medicaid. Eligibility for Medicaid, for example, has been severely eroded by being based on ever changing demographics and income levels rather than need. The current patchwork of federal and state policies on Medicaid eligibility is anything but equitable, and is in every way unfair as it stands.

Chapter Four

Perceptions and Use of the Health Care System (African–Americans) and Health Care Providers (Physicians)

Our case studies of the health care status of African Americans confirms other research on the connection between poverty, race, and health. Chapter Four focuses on African American health care users and their providers' perceptions and attitudes about their health care. Perception of the health care system is one of the other measures by which differential health care quality can be illustrated and measured. If one sector of the population had negative experiences with the health care system, this is a strong indicator that the set people is not receiving the same amount or quality of services that another may be. Perceptions of the health care system are also indirect measures of an individual or population's future health care use. In other words, if one has a bad impression of the health care system, this experience will prevent one from using the health care system even in times of need.

Today, there exists in the United States a health care delivery system where the quality of care is determined by both income and race. Income being highly correlated with race, African Americans face "double jeopardy" in the U.S. health care system. First, the structural inequalities in American society lead to greater numbers of African Americans than white Americans to be uninsured for health care. Second, because of direct overt discrimination, African Americans record lower utilization of the health care system even when insured. African Americans are significantly more likely than whites to report that during their last visit their physician did not inquire sufficiently about pain nor did the doctor tell them how long it would take for prescribed medicine. Furthermore, African Americans reported that their doctor was less likely to explain the seriousness of the illness or discuss the results of tests and possible injury or cause of death (Dressler, 1993). This differential response has been linked significantly to non-utilization of health services by African Americans because of their perception of its inefficacy.

AFRICAN-AMERICAN FOLK MEDICINE

As a consequence of their difficulty in gaining access to quality health care, the use of "folk medicine" or traditional healing practice is common among African Americans (Jackson, 1981; Watson, 1984).

The link between African American alienation and their own health behaviors has been the subject of many empirical studies. In one study, mothers who felt socially isolated and believed that they lacked the power to control their own lives or those of their children were less likely to bring their children to well-baby clinics than mothers who felt more powerful and more integrated with friends and family (Hatch,1989). Another study found that negative feelings of despair and alienation acted as barriers to mothers seeking prenatal care as well as immunizations for their children (Hatch, 1989).

These studies although old, resonated with my interviews with African Americans in Boston who expressed some distrust of the health care system. Some alluded to the Tuskegee syphilis study in which poor African American men in Alabama suffered and died of untreated syphilis in the name of science, highlighting the impact of race on health care access and treatment, and a cause for African-Americans' distrust.

A comprehensive study conducted by Krieger (1990) analyzing the pyschological barriers to preventive health care found a strong relationship between feelings of powerlessness, isolation, and hopelessness with low levels of utilization (fewer check-ups, less dental care visits, fewer immunizations, and less prenatal care. When middle class African Americans were interviewed, she discovered that despite their higher incomes, they too had experienced racial discrimination which was related to their feelings of powerlessness and hopelessness.

Given the pivotal role that psychological distress plays in health, residents of African-American neighborhoods suffer greatly from disruptions resulting from urban renewal, housing abandonment, and arson more often than those in white neighborhoods. People living in these African-American neighborhoods are often forced to leave, severing the networks of relationships that are so important for social support and mental well-being. This disruptions in turn impinges on their health especially that of the aged (Gibson and Jackson, 1987). The importance of marital and family roles as partial determinants of health was found to exist (Blendon, 1986). Furthermore, Dingle (1989) found that negative aspects of family structure and family functioning are related to a variety of indicators of poor physical and mental health ranging from mortality itself to, diabetes, cardiovascular diseases, depression and schizophrenia. They found that these family variables predict compliance with medical treatment prescriptions, help-seeking behavior, and adaptation to stress (Baugh, 1991).

The lay referral system is one of the organizational strengths of many African American communities. The concept of a lay referral system originated with Freidson (1960s), who described the usual process of seeking medical help as involving a set of potential consultants, beginning in the family, extending outward to select authoritative lay persons, and eventually reaching the "professional" practitioner (Cockerham,2004:121) Cockerham suggested that when cultural definitions of illness contradict professional ones, these lay consultants will often disagree with the mainstream medical system. Strong ethnic self-identifications and community frequently create the highest resistance to using available formal health resources.

Within the family, women are probably the most influential "medical consultants." Indeed, at the outset of a health problem within the home, the mother or wife is the one most often consulted for aid. In any case, delay in seeking medical help decreases with a wide variety of interactive variables, the most critical of which are perceived seriousness of the condition, the extent of discomfort, a belief that treatment could produce symptom abatement, and ready access to treatment. For African Americans, a long history of racism resulting in violence and exclusion, has meant that alternative system of local medicine has emerged and become central to the health care processes of the disadvantaged group. An important element of this process is lay referral systems embedded in local social networks.

If fatalism, self-treatment, and use of a lay referral system by African Americans delay the seeking of "legitimate" medical attention, then it is also true that lack of affordable and accessible formal health and medical services lengthen that delay even further often shutting patients off from treatment altogether. In fact, segregated medical facilities and other barriers to health already mentioned foster the proliferation and viability of "local" medicine in poor African-American communities (Bailey, 1991). Inadequate incomes affect many aspects of daily life that impinge on health: housing problems (rat-infested neighborhoods and overcrowding), malnutrition, the stress of struggling to make ends meet, dangerous jobs, and environmental toxins (Mantom, Patrick, and Johnson, 1987).

There has been much recent attention to how characteristics of the location of a population affects its health status (Laveist,1992). Such effects of location include lack of health resources, toxic environmental exposures, and interpersonal violence, all of which minorities, including African Americans, experience more than do white Americans.

The effect of poverty on African-American youth has detrimental health consequences that cannot be overcome despite any material gains in later life.

This is troubling when one realizes that over half of African-American children in this nation live in poverty (U.S.Bureau of Census,1991).

Another cause of poor health status is lack of health education. When compared with white Americans, African Americans on average are far less knowledgeable about coping health strategies, the health consequences of using illicit and controlled substances, and the effectiveness of prenatal care, nutrition, and other basic preventive health behaviors. Jackson (1988) asserts that maladaptive patterns of coping and hazardous forms of consumption can be seen to reflect the molding of social and cultural life by contemporary economic and race relations. Obviously, without this critical knowledge, African Americans are more susceptible to disease and illness. Yet, even African Americans who do possess preventive health knowledge may not be able to follow through because of their poverty. A simple example is that nutritional foods necessary to maintain good health are expensive and many African Americans may not have the resources to purchase such food. Another poignant example is that given by Laurie Kaye Abraham. She recounts a story of a young African-American mother with severe asthma which was exacerbated by the presence of a cat at home. The woman's doctor repeatedly asked her to give up her cat because it was adding to her health problems. But she refused. After the doctor inquired on several occasions why the woman would not get rid of the cat, she finally told the doctor that if she got rid of the cat there would be nothing to protect her children from rats (Gamble, 1994). Though health education is important, especially when most African Americans do not possess it, as this story points out, health education alone will not solve African-American health problems.

Another aspect of African-Americans lack of health education is their increased targeting by the tobacco and alcohol industry. There is of course a strong positive association between the availability of alcohol and its consumption (Feagin, 1989). Not surprisingly, fewer retail outlets are permitted to sell alcohol and tobacco in poor, minority neighborhoods than in middle class and affluent areas (LaVeist,1993). This disparity in availability is further supported by the greater use of advertising to target African Americans and Hispanics (Feagin, 1989).

Recent research also shows that because of African Americans exposure to other negative environmental conditions, both cigarette smoking and alcohol use have more adverse effects on African Americans than on white Americans (LaVeist,1992). Researchers have found that African Americans who smoke are more exposed to toxic and residential environments than their white peers; the effects of a given inadequate health practice may thus be exacerbated because of its occurrence with other risk factors.

PERCEPTIONS OF AFRICAN-AMERICANS
HEALTH CARE PROVIDERS

This section explores the perceptions of physicians as health care providers who can provide an important link to health access and health care for African Americans. Several studies (Jones and Rice, 1987; Williams,1996) have documented the important role of health care providers in influencing medical choices and access to health care.

A year-long investigation was conducted by this author at two neighborhood clinics that cater to the health needs of African Americans in Albany and Schenectady counties of up state New York. One of the clinics was the same health center as in the study of African American reported in Chapter Three of this book.

A focused sample of 10 doctors, five from each center from different specialties were interviewed. Focus groups have been used successfully as a variation on the key informant approach (Neuman, 1997) The interviews were audio-taped with permission and later transcribed. The researcher led the discussion by asking questions about the social characteristics of the patients they see, follow-up procedures, common complaints by patients and the providers' views on African-American health treatment patterns. A content analysis was performed on the transcribed tapes. This section reports findings by health care providers.

PROBLEMS WITH QUALITY OF CARE

When these doctors were asked to comment on the provision of health care services for African Americans, they overwhelmingly mentioned the problem of discontinuity of care. While most of the patients they see are on Medicaid, enrollment in Medicaid does not eliminate all the problems of access; neither does it guarantee continuity of care or high-quality care (Quaye, 1994). The majority of the doctors expressed concern about the impact of cost-control measures on the quality of care. They suggested that the use by Medicaid officials of diagnoses-related groups as well as the use of required and optional benefits have a severe impact on African Americans' access to health care. Most of the doctors reported that what is available in the American health care system for those who have limited access to or are excluded from Medicaid is the use of the hospital emergency room as their main port of entry to health care services. The doctors reported that African Americans "abuse" the emergency services by utilizing them at two local hospitals. When the respondents were asked to explain why this was the case, they overwhelmingly suggested that because African Americans have Medicaid, they feel the need to shop around for providers and the emergency room may provide one of those options. They also mentioned that some of the patients would prefer to use the emergency room since current Medicaid services do in fact cover emergency transportation but do not cover transportation to a scheduled visit at a doctor's office.

When those physicians were asked to describe what happens when a patient fails to show up for appointment (in these clinics, between 20 and 25 percent of patients do not keep their appointments), they reported that they used to send reminders through the mail. But it was difficult to reach the patient either because the patient had given a wrong address and telephone number or had moved and left no forwarding address. As one respondent stated, "They move so often and without warning that you have no clue as to what happened to them." Currently, the two clinics each have an outreach department whose primary responsibilities are to call and remind patients 24 hours before their scheduled appointments, and to follow up when they do not show up and fail to reschedule their appointments. The outreach departments face the same problem of incorrect addresses. When these medical respondents were asked whether there are special cultural differences in practices and attitudes among African Americans in utilization of health services, half of the doctors from each clinic mentioned that African-American patients were likely to be influenced by other members of their family, particularly grandmothers and aunts. Two respondents mentioned that all their African-American patients "tend to delay seeking treatment and tend to use home remedies."

When providers were asked to suggest specific ways of improving health care for African Americans, they overwhelmingly, suggested that great effort should be devoted to preventive medicine. They wanted African American parents to show up for routine preventive services, such as immunizations for their children and reduced use of hospital emergency rooms as their primary access to the health care system.

The physicians also urged that African Americans rate for showing up at scheduled appointments be improved by encouraging African Americans to select a single provider to ensure continuity of care. Most of the doctors suggested that the current health care system is badly broken and must be fixed.

As one doctor put it, "They need someone like a social worker, with education in health promotion in the community." They all concluded that a health-maintenance organization (HMO) style system with a combined fee-for service and capitation payment systems might be an important way to overcome barriers African Americans face in accessing the American health care system.

CONCLUSION

What is clear from the physicians' responses is that the current U.S. health care system, based on a mixture of private insurance and public programs with strict eligibility requirements (age, income, health and family status) has not solved the problem of access (OECD, 1992).

At any given time, about fifteen percent of the entire U.S. population has no health insurance. As already pointed out, among African Americans the percentage is 22 percent (Kuttner, 1999). Given the Americas employment based insurance system, African Americans with weak connections to the labor market have a high probability of being uninsured. Given this the aborted Clinton health care plan could be reconsidered by Congress as a bold attempt in fill gaps in the financing and delivery of health services. Clinton's Health Security Act was grounded in six basic principles: security, simplicity, savings, quality, choice, and responsibility (The White House Domestic Policy Council, 1993). A focus of that proposal was managed care, which was expected to encourage competition among health care providers; health consumers would join large purchasing groups powerful enough to bargain with HMOs for lower cost. But everyone would be required to pay more money than in insurance premiums (Bodenheimer, 1993) by reducing health care costs by encouraging and expanding community-based health alliances through HMOs. This would no doubt address, to some extent, the problems of the uninsured. After all, better health contributes to economic security by permitting persons to earn more income and by reducing financial expenditure arising from health needs (Schiller, 1998). Such optimistic results might be possible, provided Congress guarantees universal health care for all Americans.

In any case, the current caps on health spending will undoubtedly force a debate on rationing of health care. The test case may the State of Oregon's basic health act of 1991 which guarantees health insurance coverage for the uninsured in Oregon by singling out the most vulnerable—poor women and children to benefit most from the services (Strosberg et al. 1992). In other countries, attempts to control costs have almost always led to some form of rationing, delay and even denial of health care services. It is quite clear that in effect the United States is rationing health care for the over forty-three million uninsured Americans.

So what can be done? It is to these specific issues that we now turn.

Chapter Five

Agenda for Reform

It is clear from our discussion that any attempt to improve the health of African Americans should resolve the central issue of equity in health care, and therefore by implication, address both the racial and class determinants of health. The equity problem is a problem of ensuring that no individual who has the bad luck of getting sick for financial reasons be denied a decent standard of care (Blomqvist, 1979). Because health care in the United States is mostly accessed through an employer-based insurance system as we have repeatedly pointed out, African Americans with weak access to the labor market are much more likely to suffer the ill-effects of being uninsured for health care. For this reason, we need to start considering either expanding Medicaid for the poor or providing tax credits to help families meet their health care needs. We also need to consider rectifying current unequal educational opportunities as ways of overcoming African Americans' disadvantages in the U.S. labor market. Inequality of educational opportunities across income classes tends to be reinforced by the way schools are financed. Over half of all elementary and secondary school expenditures are supported by local property taxes (Schiller, 2004). The implication is clear. Children in poorer communities are denied adequate educational resources. Such schools are more likely to pay teachers less, and therefore to attract poorly prepared teachers. Furthermore, they usually lack up-to-date instructional technology. This is why study upon study cited earlier has consistently shown that students in suburban American schools do better educationally than their counterparts in poorer areas. Thus an important barrier to education is average family income. Of all high-income ($50,000 per year). 56.4 percent have at least one child in college, while among the lowest-income families making (under $10,000 a year), only 15.3 percent have a child in college. Furthermore the economic status of one's family has a significant impact on a child's chance for a college education (Schiller, 2004). With a poverty rate (33 percent) three times that of whites (11 percent), African Americans are less likely to have children in college.

There are underlying reasons for the higher percentage of poverty-stricken African Americans. For example, trends in the labor market create and consistently maintain a certain proportion of low-paying, unstable jobs (Gilbert and Kahl,1993). Using the labor market segmentation theory, Piore (1979) suggests that those who enter the labor market with only a secondary school education are more likely to be paid lower wages, work under poorer conditions, and experience much less opportunity for advancement.

To explain why the working poor fall on the wrong side of this divide, Gilbert and Kahl (1993) offered two explanations. First, the structure of job opportunities offered by the U.S. economy and, second, the relative standing of workers, attitudes of employers, and the effect of social networking have major implications for the wage-earnings of African Americans.

Yet, while level of education generally predicts level of income and, by implication, social standing, any given amount of education yields greater economic returns to white males than either women or African Americans (Schiller, 2004). In 1990, the average yearly earnings of college-educated African American men were only 73 percent of the earnings of their white counterparts (Gilbert and Kahl, 2000). Thus discrimination acts to retard African American educational progress as well as their labor market success.

Even with increased availability of health services and the promotion of their utilization through Medicaid, there are still numerous factors inhibiting access and use of health services. While the Medicaid program is supposed to constitute a safety net for those who become poor, this is not the case for large numbers of the poor. In reality, of poor families with income one and a quarter below the poverty line, 27 percent are completely uninsured (Friedman, 1995).

In fact non-participation by private physicians in health care for African Americans is also of concern. Access to physicians with specialized knowledge and training is especially critical and should be of a major concern for African Americans who are at high risk and live in the urban and especially the inner areas. As is well documented (Komaromy et al. 1996:) white physicians are less likely to practice in inner city areas than are African American or Hispanic doctors. The study concluded that, "On average, African-American physicians practiced in area with more African-American residents than did other physicians (14 percent vs. 6 percent, P. <0.001), and Hispanic physicians practiced in areas with more Hispanic residents than did other physicians"(1308). This increasingly, minority physicians (especially blacks and Hispanics) are more likely to practice in urban areas. Yet the proportion of trained minority physicians in the United States is only about 5 percent of the total number of doctors graduating from medical schools. To overcome the shortage of inner-city physicians there needs to be a national commitment to encourage and to aggressively institute affirmative action programs in medical schools to ensure greater enrollment of African Americans in medical schools. This would be one important way to addressing the lack of access that African Americans face in the health care system.

The dysfunctions of African-American health care can be seen in the chronic diseases that pervade this population and account for its high morbidity and mortality rates. Heart disease, one of the primary results of untreated and undiagnosed high blood pressure, is taking a toll. As already noted, hypertension and its complications are the single most important factors in the gap between African Americans and whites.

Of the 60 million people in the United States with some type of hypertension, 7 million are African Americans. Within the United States, hypertension is more common among the poor, those living in high-crime areas (LaVeist,1992). Such epidemiological observations refute any unifactorial etiological hypotheses by which modernization and its accompanying stresses become causative.

Medical response to hypertension—a socially mutable disease—has been dominated by the economic imperatives of capital. That is, research has now been shaped towards therapies requiring the production of health care commodities and the making of profits for firms by selling such products. More than two hundred drugs have been marketed in the United States for treatment of hypertension; yet the total research in non-pharmacological interventions is probably less than the cost of developing a single new drug. Biomedical specialists concentrate on politically safe profit-maximizing, without paying greater attention to the American health care consumer. The grim reality of African-American health should be an anachronism in a wealthy society as United States. It is a sad indictment that the health of an African American in the army or in prison is considerably better than the health of one in urban America (Angier, 1990:3).

Racism is at the root of poor health for African Americans. The longer it remains unresolved, the longer the preventable and treatable health problems of African Americans will persist and thus the poorer their health will be. True health care reform starts with surveying shortcomings of the nation's health care system. Spending on health care has risen from less than 6 percent of the gross national product in 1964 to 14 percent in 2000 (Kuttner,1999). At the end of the last century, health care costs were projected to be 17 percent of GDP and 37 percent by the year 2030 (Kuttner, 1999) yet, although most of the federal budget for health care goes to Medicare and Medicaid (34%), there has not been expansion of adequate coverage to those who persistently remain uninsured. In reality, with nearly hundred hospitals closing each year across the country and the cost of treating the uninsured increasing, while federal health subsidies continue to be inadequate, hospitals have increasingly turned away the uninsured (Taira and Taira, 1991).

Good public health policy would mandate basic priorities and levels of funding for primary health care. These should not change from one administration to another. The population most dependent on public health services are the ones most likely to lose confidence and any desire to participate in such a system thus marginalizing them and their health care. Cost-effective prevention and treatment programs must be established. But beyond these, access to good health, financial, geographic and racial can be effectively overcome if resources are distributed in a more equitable manner.

This may seem impossible in a society where race so determines socioeconomic status and thereby influences treatment by the biomedical health care system. The implementation of race–specific policies that address particular problems faced by African Americans is critical for getting at the root of U.S. health care service inequities. Since race has been a significant factor in the structuring of health care delivery, health policies that address the issue of class, exclusive of race, will effectively marginalize, as it does now, not only the large population of poor African Americans but even those of medium incomes As it stands, less attention has been paid to the racial barriers to health and health care. Instead, class-based solutions are chosen completely disregarding the extensive data demonstrating that simply equalizing the ability to pay for care does not eliminate racial discrimination in the distribution and availability of health care resources.

But health is multifaceted. It does not depend merely on health care! Far from it. Good health habits must be embedded in people's lives from the start. To simply change health care approaches alone is to use a band-aid approach when "radical surgery" is needed.

The nation needs a health care system that guarantees basic coverage to all Americans. If Canada, Great Britain, Sweden and the Netherlands can have developed health care systems where race, class, age and gender are not barriers to care, why not the United States? One cannot believe that we are not able to provide affordable health care for all Americans. Making coverage possible and easy for all Americans to get should be the hallmark of any comprehensive health care reform. How long can we ignore the uninsured and still hold on to our ideals of equal opportunity and access in a land of plenty? Investing now in our health care system is nothing more than an investment in the future. Countries that have provided universal health care coverage for all their citizens have realized the massive health care cost savings associated with such a policy. As we in the United States struggle to contain health care costs, it is time to recognize that tax incentives for health care coverage only to big corporations will in the long run not be in the best interests of this country. As has been demonstrated, the loss of manufacturing jobs overseas and the high cost of prescription drugs in the face of a potentially bankrupt Medicaid and Medicare systems will in the end frustrate the aspirations of younger and older Americans. The time to act is now, and act we must.

But in the meantime, perhaps a new approach to health care delivery may offer better access to care for poor people. As studies indicate, "Several health care organizations have enlisted the support of African-Americans churches in efforts to reach the African American community." (Hatch, 1989:1). Since religion and church membership are central to many in African American communities, the value of using the churches as centers for health promotion cannot be denied. As observed by Hatch (1989:17) "the gap between health care providers and the community can be narrowed through an equal exchange of expertise and ideas on how to reach the African-American community." The established monthly blood pressure screening after Sunday services, an infant–seat-restraint loan program, parenting programs to train teenage mothers in pre- and post-natal care, and training on dental care have proven to be a useful vehicle for improving the health care status of African Americans. Church-based health projects in North and South Carolina should be duplicated in African American communities as they have worked effectively to reduce risks of selected health problems through increased knowledge, life style changes and more accessible and appropriate utilization of health services (Hatch, 1989). This is the American challenge and there is evidence that it will succeed.

Appendix A

This is an exploratory research examining health seeking behavior among African Americans. If you would take a few minutes to fill out these questions as accurately as possible, it would be highly appreciated.

A. *Socio-Demographic Data*
    1. Sex   Male ___   Female ___
    2. Age   20–25   26–31   32–36   36– or specify ___
    3. Marital Status: Married ___ Single ___ Divorced ___
        Cohabitation ___ Gay parent ___ Widowed ___ Other ___
    4. How many children do you have? ___

B. *Jobs/Income*
    5. What do you do to support yourself and your family?
        Own your own business ___ . Work for the state ___ .
        State employee ___ City ___ County ___ unemployed ___
        Other _____ .

C. *Education*
    7. What is the highest educational level attained?
        High School ___
        Vocational ___
        Undergraduate ___
        No Schooling ___
        Graduate ___
        Adult Education currently enrolled (years) ___

D. *Religion*
    8.   Are you religious? Yes ____ No ____ .
    9.   Do you belong to a church? Yes ____ No ____ . If yes, what church do
        you go to? _____ .
   10. Who is the breadwinner of the family? Both of couple ____
        or one ____
E. *Sickness Behavior*
   11. What has been the common health complaint by you? _____
        or by members of your family? _____
   12. Do you believe in faith or traditional forms of healing? _____
 12a. Name them _____
   13. Do you believe in faith and prayer as healing tools?
        Yes ____ No ____ Other _____
        To what extent is your decision to seek medical help shaped by your
        beliefs?
        Always ____ Sometimes ____ Not at all ____
F. *Choice of Therapy*
   14. Whom do you see when you or members of your family get sick?
        Doctor (physician) ____ Psychologist ____ or Psychiatrist ____
        Friend ____ Priest ____ Healer ____ Other _____
   15. Who makes this decision concerning the choice of therapy?
        You ____ Relative ____ Other _____
   16. Where do you go for treatment?
        Clinic ____ Church ____ Doctor's office ____ Emergency room ____
        Hospital (specify type) _____
   17.
   18. Who pays for the service?
        Yourself ____ Relatives ____ Private insurance ____ Medicaid ____
        Medicare ____ Employer ____ Other _____
   19. How often do you see your health care practitioner? _____
   20. What has been your experience with these health care providers?
        (describe briefly)

        _____

        _____

        _____

        _____

   21. Under what circumstance (s) have you not sought medical help
        when sick?
        (describe why) _____

        _____

        _____

22. Are you familiar with president Clinton's health care proposal?
    Yes ___ No ___

23. What are some of the key aspects of Clinton's health proposal?

    _____

    _____

24. Do you feel this proposal, if passed, will improve your access to health car?
    Yes ___ No ___ Other _____

25. Are you involved with the African American community?
    Yes ___ No ___
    If yes, specify your role in the community. _____

26. What causes sickness from your understanding? _____

    _____ .

27. Do you believe in other force (Spirit or Power) of healing?
    Yes ___ No ___

28. Do you draw distinction between different aspects of illness.
    Yes ___ No ___ .

Bibliography

Aguirre, Adalberto Jr., and Jonathan Turner. *American Ethnicity: The Dynamics and Consequences of Discrimination* Boston, Ma.: McGraw Hill, 2004.

Alliance for Health Reform: *Health Care Coverage in America*. Washington, D.C.: Robert Wood Johnson Foundation, 2004.

Anderson, Elijah. *Street Wise: Race, Class, and Change in an Urban Community*. Chicago, IL.: The University of Chicago Press, 1990.

Armas, Genardo. "Poverty up for Second straight year." *Daily Record*, 27 September 2003, 104: 111–112).

Arnason, Wayne B. "Directed Donation: The Relevance of Race," *Hastings Center Report* 21, (1991):13–19.

Ayarian, John B. "Disease in Black and White." *New England Journal of Medicine* 329, (1993):656–658.

Auletta, Ken. *The Underclass*. New York, New York: Random House, 1982.

Aday, Lu Ann. "The Impact of Health Policy on Access to Medical Care. "*Milbank Memorial Fund Quarterly*" 65, no.1 (1987):149–176.

Aday, Lu Ann. " The National Profile of Access to Medical Care: Where Do We Stand?" *American Journal of Public Health* 74, (1986):1331–1339.

Angier, Natalie. Folk Beliefs play role in taking medication," *New York Times*, 23 October 1990:3–4

Bailey, Eric J. "Hypertension: An Analysis of Detroit African-American Health Care Treatment Patterns." *Human Organization* 50 (1991):287–296.

Baldwin, Marjorie L. and William Johnson "The Employment Effects of Wage Discrimination Against Black Men." *Industrial and Labor Relations Review* 49, (1996):302–316.

Baugh, Joyce A. "African Americans and the Environment: Review Essay." *Policy Studies Journal* 19, (1991):182–191.

Beardsley, Edward H. *A History of Neglect: Health Care for Black Mill Workers in the Twentieth-Century South*. Tenn: The University of Tennessee Press, 1987.

Belgrave, Linda L. and Julia Bradsher "Health as a Factor in Institutionalization Disparities between African Americans and Whites." *Research on Aging* 16(1994):115–41.

Belgrave, Linda L., May L.Wykle and Jung M. Choi. "Health Double Jeopardy, and Culture: The Use of Institutionalization by African Americans." *American Journal of Sociology* 33, (1993):379–85.

Becker, Lawrence. "Race, Health and Health Services." *American Journal of Public Health* 83, (1993):939–941.

Boston, Thomas D. "Segmented Labor Markets: New Evidence from a Study of Four Race-Gender Groups." *Industrial and Labor Relations Review* 44, (1990):99–115

Blendon, RJ, Aiken, L.H., Freeman, H.E., Corey, C.R. "Access to Medical Care for Black and White Americans: A Matter of Continuing Concern." *Journal of American Medical Association*, 261 (1989):278–291.

Blendon, R. J. " Health Policy Choices for the 1990s." *Issues in Science and Technology*, 2 (1986):65–73.

Blomqvist, Ake. *The Health Care Business*. London, Ontario: The Fraser Institute, 1979.

Bodenheimer, Thomas. " The Health Care Game," *Nation*, March 22 1993.

Bonsi, Stephen K. "Traditional Medical Practice in Modern Ghana." Ann Arbor, MI 1974:1–162 (Unpublished Doctoral Dissertation).

Coplan, Arthur L. " When Evil Intrudes." *Hastings Center Report* 22, (1992):29–32.

Cockerham, William. *Medical Sociology*. Upper Saddle River, NJ.: Prentice Hall, 2004.

Council on Ethical and Judicial Affairs, AMA. " Black-white Disparities in Health Care." *Journal of American Medical Association* 262 (1990):2344–2346.

Conyors, John. "Principles of Healthcare Reform: An African-American Perspective." *Journal of Health Care for the Poor and Underserved* 4 (1993):242–249.

Commonwealth Fund Task Force on Academic Health Centers. " *A Shared Responsibility; Academic Health Centers and the Provision of Care to the Poor and Uninsured*. The Common wealth Fund, 2001.

Davis, Karen, Anderson, Gerard, Rowland, Diane, Steinberg, Earl. *Health Care Cost Containment*. Baltimore, Md.; John Hopkins University Press, 1990, 182–199.

Davis, Karen and Rowland, D. "Health Care for Black Americans: The Public Sector Role, *Milbank Quarterly* 65 (1987):213–47.

Davis, Karen. "Inequality and Access to Health Care." *Milbank Quarterly* 69 (1991):253–73.

Dervarics, Charles. "Landmark Study Confirms Widespread Job Bias; All Things Being Equal, White Males Are Still Preferred." *Black Issues in Higher Education* 8 (1991): 1–12.

Dingle, Derek T. "An Agenda for the Black Middle Class." *Black Enterprise* 20 (1989):52–60.

Dressler, William W. "Health in the African American Community: *Accounting for Health Irregularity." Medical Anthropology* Quarterly 7 (1993):325–45.

Dula, Annette and Sara Goering. It Just Ain't Fair: *The Ethics of Health Care For African Americans.* Westport, CT.; Praeger, 1994.

Ell, Kathleen, L., Julian Haywood and Eugene Sobel. "Acute Chest Pain in African Americans: Factors in the Delay in Seeking Emergency Care." *American Journal of Public Health* 84(1994):965–970.

Eggers, P. "Beneficiary Impact of the Medicare Prospective Payment Systems" (paper presented to the Villers Foundation Roundtable, Washington, D. C., December 13 1985).

Frank, Richard. "Updated Estimates of the Impact of Prenatal Care on Birth Weight Outcomes by Race." *The Journal of Human Resources* 27 (1992):629–642.

Friedman, Emily. "Medicare and Medicaid After 30 Years." *Journal of American Medical Association* 274 (1995):278–282.

Friedman, Emily. "The Uninsured: From Dilemma to Crisis." *Journal of American Medical Association* 265 (1991):2491–2495.

Friedson, Elliot. "Client Control and Medical Practice." *American Journal of Sociology* 65 (1960):374–382.

Fetter, D.,Brand, D., and Gamache, D., eds., *DRGs: Their Design and Development.* Ann Arbor, Mi.: Health Administration Press, (1991), 207–233

Feagin, J.R. *Racial and Ethnic Relations*, 3rd ed. Englewood Cliffs, New Jersey, Prentice Hall, 1989.

Gamble, Vanessa. "The Politics of Health: Race Blindness in D. C.?" *Dissent* 41 (1994):200–203.

Gilbert, Dennis and Kahl, Joseph. *The American Class Structure* (Belmont, CA,: Wadsworth Publishing Company, (1993), 4–18.

Gibson, R. C. and Jackson, J.S. " The Health, Physical Functioning, and Informal Supports of the Black Elderly." *Milbank Quarterly* 63 (1987):206–285.

Geiger, Jack. "Race and Health Care—An American Dilemma?" *New England Journal of Medicine* 335 (1996):815–816.

Gormick, M., Eggers, P., Reilly, T., Mentnech,R., Fitterman, L., Kucken, La and Vladeck, B. "Effects of Race and Income on Mortality and Use of Services Among Medicare Beneficiaries." *New England Journal of Medicine* 335 (1996):791–799.

Goldberg, K., Hartz, R., Jacobson, S., KraKauser, H., and Rimm, A. "Racial and Community Factors Influencing Coronary Artery By pass Graft Surgery Rates for All 1986 Medicare Patients." *Journal of American Medical Association* 267 (March 1992):1473–1477.

Hadley, Jack,, Steinberg, Earl and Feder, Judith, "Comparison of Uninsured and Privately *Insured Hospital Patients." Journal of American Medical Association* 263 (1991):374–379.

Hatch, J. " The Church as a Resource for Health Promotion Activity in the Black Community." (Paper presented at the Carter Center of Emory University, Atlanta, GA., April 1989), 1–10.

James, Sherman A."John Henryism and the Health of African–Americans." *Culture, Medicine and Psychiatry* 18 (1994):163–82.

Jackson, J. S. (ed).*The Black American Elderly: Research on Physical and Psychological Health.* Springer, New York, 1988.

Jones, Woodrow Jr, and Mitchell F. Rice. *Health Care Issues in Black America* Westport, CT.: Greenwood Press, 1987.

Kasiske, Bertram, "The Effects of Race on Access and Outcomes in Transplantation." *New England Journal of Medicine* 324 (1991):302–07.

Johnson, John M. *Doing Field Research.* New York: Free Press, 1975.

Komaromy, M.,Grumbach, K., Drake. M., Vranzan,K., Lure,N., Keane, D. and Bindman, A. "The Role of Black and Hispanic Physicians in providing Health Care for Underserved Populations. "*The New England Journal of Medicine*, 334, no.20 (May 1996):1305–1310.

Kjellstrand, Carl M. "Age, Sex and Race Inequality in Renal Transplantation." *Archives of Internal Medicine* 148 (1988):1305–1309.

Kjellstrand, C.M. and Kogan, M. " Age, Sex and Race Inequality in Renal Transplantation." *Archives of Internal Medicine* 148 (1987):1305–1309.

Kogan, Michael, Kotelchuc, M., Alexander, G.R., and Johnson, W.E. "Racial Disparities in Reported Prenatal Care Advice from Health Care Provider." American Journal of Public Health 84 (1994):82–88.

Krieger, Nancy and Mary Bassett. "The Health of Black Folk: Disease, Class, and Ideology in Science. "*Monthly Review* 38 (1986):74–85.

Krieger, Nancy. "Racial and Gender Discrimination: Risk Factors for High Blood Pressure." *Social Science and Medicine* 30 (1990):1273–81.

Kuttner, Robert. "The American Health Care. "*The New England Journal of Medicine* 340 (1999) no.2:163–168.

LaVeist, Thomas A. "The Political Empowerment and Health Status of African Americans: Mapping a New Territory." *American Journal of Sociology* 97 (1992):1080–1095.

LaVeist, Thomas A. "Segregation, Poverty, and Empowerment: Health Consequences for African Americans." Milbank Quarterly 71 (1993):41–64.

Lieu, T. A., Newacheck, P. W., McManus, M. A. "Race, Ethnicity and Access to Ambulatory Care Among U.S. Adolescents." *American Journal of Public Health* 83 (1993):960–965.

Lewin, Arthur. " A Tale of Two Classes: The Black Poor and the Black Middle Class." *The Black Scholar* 21 (1991):7–13.

Massey, Douglas S. and Kumiko Shibuya. "Unraveling the Tangle of Pathology: The Effect of Spatially Concentrated Joblessness on the Well-Being of African Americans." *Social Science Research* 24 (1995):352–366.

Massey Douglas and Nancy Denton. *America Apartheid: Segregation and the Making of the Underclass*. Boston, Mass.: Harvard University Press,1993.

McKenzie, Nancy F. *Beyond Crisis: Confronting Health Care in the United States* New York.: Penguin, 1994.

Mincy, R. B. " Paradoxes in Black Economic Progress: Income, Families and the Underclass." *Journal of Negro Education* 58 (1989):255–269.

Manton, K. G., Patrick, C.H., and Johnson, K. W. "Health Differentials Between Blacks and Whites." *Milbank Quarterly* 65, 1 (1987):129–199.

Miller, S. M. "Race in the Health of America." *Milbank Quarterly* 65, 1 (1987):111–116.

McDonald,Thomas and Andrew Coburn. "Predictors of Prenatal Care Utilization." *Social Science and Medicine* 27, 2 (1988):167–172.

National Health Interview Survey. *Healthy 2000 Report*. Hyattsville,Md.: Department of Health and Human Services,1990.

Neuman, Lawrence. *Social Research Methods*. Boston, Mass.: Allyn and Bacon, 1997.

Organization For Economic Cooperation and Development. *U.S. Health Care At The Cross-Roads*. Paris, France: Health Policy Studies No.1, 1992.

Piore, Michael." The Dual Labor Market and Its Implications," In Problems in Political Economy: An Urban Perspective, D.C. Heath, 1977

Quaye, Randolph. "The Health Care Status of African Americans." *The Black Scholar* 24 (1994):12–18.

Quaye. Randolph. "Health Care in Black America: Perceptions of Users in a Negotiated Order." *Journal of Multicultural Nursing and Health* 9 no.2 (2003):1–9.

Roux, Ana, Meekin, Sharon, Arnett, Donna,Chambless, Lloyd, Massing, Mark, Nieto, Javier, Sorlie, Paul, Szklo, Moyses, Tyroller, Herman and Watson, Robert "Neighborhood of Residence and Incidence of Coronary Heart Disease. "*The New England Journal of Medicine* 345, no.2 (July 2001):99–106.

Rosenback,Margo. " The Impact of Medicaid on Physician Use by Low-Income Children." *American Journal of Public Health*,79 (1989):1220–1226.

Rothman, Robert. *Inequality and Stratification*. New Jersey: Prentice Hall, 1993.

Reed. Alyson. " Trends in State Laws and Regulation Affecting Nurse-Midwives." *Journal of Nurse-Midwifery* 42 (1992):421–426.

Strogatz, D. "Use of Medical Care for Chest Pain Differences Between Blacks and Whites. *American Journal of Public Health*," 80 (March 1990):290–294.

Schulman. Kevin., Berlin, Jesse, Harless, William., Kerner, Jon, Sistrunk, Shyrl, Gersh, Eisenberg and Escarce, Jose. "The Effect of Race and Sex on Physicians' Recommendations for Cardiac Catheterization." *The New England Journal of Medicine* 340: (1999):618–626.

Saver, Barry G. and Nancy Peterfreund. "Insurance, Income, and Access to Ambulatory Care in King County, Washington." American Journal of Public Health 83 (1993):1583–1588.

Schiller, Bradley. R. *The Economics of Poverty and Discrimination.* Englewood Cliffs, NJ.: Prentice Hall, 1998.

Susser,M. Watson, W. and Hopper, K. *Sociology in Medicine.* New York: Oxford University Press, 1985.

Schiller, Bradley R. *The Economics of Poverty and Discrimination.* Englewood Cliffs, NJ.: Prentice Hall, 2004.

Steinberg, Stephen. "The Underclass: A Case of Color Blindness." New Politics 2 (1989):42–60.

Strosberg, Martin, Weiner, Joshua, Baker, Robert. And Fein Alan. *Rationing America's Medical Care: The Oregon Plan and Beyond.* Washington. D. C.: The Brookings Institution, 1992.

Sullivan, L.W. "From the Secretary of Health and Human services: Effects of Discrimination and Racism on Access to Health Care." *Journal of American Medical Association*, (1991):2266–2674.

Frances Taira and Deborah Taira. "Patient 'Dumping' of Poor Families," *Families in Society* (September 1991):409–415.

Temkin-Greener, Helena and Kathryn Clark. " Ethnicity, Gender, and Utilization of Mental Health Services in a Medicaid Population," *Social Science and Medicine* 26, no.10 (1988):989–996.

Tierney, William. " Effect of Hypertension and Type II Diabetes on Renal Function in an Urban Population." *American Journal of Hypertension* 3, no.1 (January 1990):69–76

U. S. Department of Health and Human Services. *Public Health Services: Health Resources and Services* Washington. D.C. Government Printing Office, 1992.

U.S. Bureau of Census *Schenectady County.* Schenectady, NY. U.S. Government Printing Office, 1992.

U. S. Bureau of Census. *Boston City.* Boston, Mass. U. S. Government Printing Office, 1992.

U.S. Bureau of Census. *The Black Population in the United States.* Washington, D.C., U.S. Government Printing Office, 1991.

U.S. Congressional Budget Office. *The Economic Status of African Americans* Washington, D. C. U.S. Government Printing Office, 1989.

VanHorne, Winston, A. and Thomas Tonnesen (eds). *Ethnicity and Health.* Wisconsin: University of Wisconsin System, 1988.

Wright, Jackson, T. "Profile of Systematic Hypertension in Black Patients." *American Journal of Cardiology* 61, No16 (1988):41–45.

Wallace, Deborah. "Roots of Increased Health Care Inequality in New York." *Social Science and Medicine* 31 (1990):1219–1227.

Warren, Mark R. "Racism and the Underclass." *Research in Race and Ethnic Relations* 8 (1995):77–97.

Williams, David. "Racism and Health: A Research Agenda." *Ethnicity and Disease* 6 (1996): 23–27.

William, David, R., Yan Yu, James Jackson, S., and Anderson, N.B." Racial Differences in Physical and Mental Health: Socio-Economic Status, Stress and Discrimination." *Journal of Health Psychology* 2 (1997):335–351.

White-Means, Shelley I. and Michael Thornton. "Non-Emergency Visits to Hospital Emergency Rooms: A Comparison of Blacks and Whites." *The Milbank Quarterly* 67 (1989):35–57.

White House Domestic Policy Council. *The President's Health Security Plan*. Washington. D.C. Government Printing Office,1993.

Weber, Max. *The Theory of Social and Economic Organization* New York. Oxford University Press, 1947.

Wilson, Julius. *The Truly Disadvantaged*. Chicago, Chicago University Oress, 1987.

Yetman, Norman. *Majority and Minority: The Dynamics of Race and Ethnicity in American Life*. Boston, Mass.: Allyn and Bacon, 1991.

Index

Abraham, Laurie Kaye, 42
access to health care. *See* health care
  utilization
Aday, 14, 18, 19
African Americans. *See also specific topics:*
  beliefs regarding health care, 28–29, 30,
  32, 33; churches as centers for health
  promotion, 51; community, 40–41;
  family, 40–41; perception of health care
  system, 39–42; prayer, 28, 32
African Americans, the National Health
  Interview Survey, 25–26
Aguirre, Adalberto, Jr., vii, 6
Aid to Families with Dependent
  Children (AFDC), 17
air pollution, 25
alcoholism, 42
Alliance for Health Reform, viii
Anderson, Elijah, 25
anger coping, 23
angioplasty, 14
appointments, 44
Armas, Genardo, 1
asthma, 42
Auletta, Ken, 4

Bailey, Eric J., 2, 28, 41
Bassett, Mary, 7, 23
Baugh, Joyce A., 41

Berger , 2
Berlin, Jesse, 2
blaming the victim, 4
Blendon, R. J., 3, 12, 13, 40
Blomqvist, Ake, 47
blood pressure, 21, 49
Bodenheimer, Thomas, 45
Bonsi, Stephen K., 28
Boston area research project, 27–29
By pass surgery, 14, 15, 36

cardiac catheterization, 15
chemo dialysis, 14
chest pain, 12
chronic disease, 49
Clark, Kathryn, 19
Clinton's Health Security Act, 45
Cockerham, William, 2, 20, 41
College of Wooster: Faculty
  Development Fund, v
Commonwealth Fund Task Force on
  Academic Health Centers, 14
coronary angiography, 14, 15
coronary artery graft bypass (CAGB).
  See bypass surgery
Council on Ethical and Judicial Affairs
  of the American Medical
  Association, 12, 14
culture of poverty thesis, 3–4

Davis, Karen, 13, 16, 18, 19, 29, 34
Denton, Nancy, 6
diabetes, 1, 23–24
diabetes mellitus, 2
Diagnosis Related Groups (DRGs), 18
Dingle, Derek T. 40
Doing Field Research (Johnson), 32
Dorchester. *See* Boston area research
    project

economic class, 4–6, 34, 35; class,
    definition of, 4
economic discrimination, 5; labor
    market discrimination *vs.* non-labor
    market discrimination, 7
economic system, U. S., 1–9
education, 6, 8, 47; African American
    vs. white levels of, 7; discrimination,
    11; level of education and
    hypertension, 23
elderly, viii, 16–17
Ell, Kathleen, 2
emergency rooms, 2, 13, 35, 43–44
employment issues: education and, 48;
    family income, 6; income gaps, 5–6,
    47–48; job discrimination, 11; labor
    market, 48; occupational distribution,
    5; unemployment, 6, 24–25
environmental factors, 24–25
Escarce, Jose, 2

fatalism, 41
Feagin, J. R., 42
feminization of poverty, 1
Fetter, D., 19
folk medicine, 2, 28, 40–42
Friedman, Emily, 5, 16, 20, 36, 48
Friedson, Elliot, 41

Gamble, Vanessa, 42
Gibson, 40
Gilbert, Dennis, 4, 48
Goldberg, K., 14, 36

Harless, William, 2
Hartz, R., 14

Hatch, J., 40, 51
Haywood, Julian, 2
health care coverage, vii, 50–51;
    churches as centers for health
    promotion, 51; discontinuity of care,
    43
health care financing, vii
health care providers, perceptions of,
    43–44
health care quality, 13–14, 43–44. *See
    also specific issues*
health care utilization, 12–13, 29, 35;
    adolescents, 12; children, 12; port of
    entry, 13, 19, 29, 35, 43–44; social
    class, 34; women, 12–13
health education, 22, 42
health insurance, viii, 11, 29, 45;
    African American *vs.* white
    coverage, 16; "patient dumping," 14
health-maintenance organization
    (HMO), 44, 45
health reform, 47–51; Clinton's Health
    Security Act, 45; equity issues, 47
health-seeking behavior, 27–37
health status, 11, 27
heart disease, 49. *See also* bypass
    surgery
Hopper, 20
hospital discharge rates, 2
hospitals: hospitalization rates, 19;
    private, 19
housing issues, 8; residential
    segregation, 6, 24
hypertension, 4, 21–23, 49; level of
    education and hypertension, 23

infant mortality rates, v, vii, 1
institutional discrimination, 9, 39
intensive care, 14
interviews: African Americans, 27, 28,
    53–55; health care providers, 43

Jackson, 4, 25, 40, 42
Jacobson, S., 14
James, Sherman A., 22
Jaynes, 7, 8